Women's Quest
for Economic Equality

D0732319

WOMEN'S QUEST
for Economic Equality

Victor R. Fuchs

Harvard University Press
Cambridge, Massachusetts
London, England

First Harvard University Press paperback edition, 1990

Library of Congress Cataloging-in-Publication Data

Fuchs, Victor R.
  Women's quest for economic equality / Victor R. Fuchs.
     p.   cm.
  Bibliography: p.
  Includes index.
  ISBN 0-674-95545-5 (alk. paper) (cloth)
  ISBN 0-674-95546-3 (paper)
  1. Women—United States—Economic conditions.   2. Women—
Employment—United States. 3. United States—Social policy—1980–
I. Title.
HQ1426.F87 1988   88–7209
305.4'2'0973—dc19   CIP

To Bev

Acknowledgments

Many people helped me bring this book to fruition and I am happy to have this opportunity to express my gratitude to them.

The foundations that supported my research deserve a special note of thanks. When I finished *How We Live* (1983), an analysis of problems relating to family, work, health, and education over the life cycle, several issues seemed to me to require further study. The most important of these concerned gender—the changing roles and relationships of women and men during the past quarter-century and the evidence of continuing economic inequality. Both my own analysis and those of others seemed incomplete, and the policy discussions often appeared misdirected. I approached several foundations in order to obtain research support, but was unsuccessful. One staff person told me that the "women's issue" was a dead topic. Another said that the answers were all known. Fortunately, my next two stops were at the Alfred P. Sloan Foundation and the Rockefeller Foundation, where the officers and trustees shared my view that the issues were important and complex. I am delighted to thank Albert Rees and Arthur Singer of the Sloan Foundation, and Richard Lyman and Phoebe Cottingham of the Rockefeller Foundation, for providing the encouragement and the funding that made this work possible.

The National Bureau of Economic Research, my research base for more than twenty-five years, continued to offer a congenial and productive setting for me and my colleagues. Conscientious, capable research assistants processed a vast amount of data,

tracked down obscure sources in the libraries, and helped prepare
the tables and figures. Joyce Jacobsen had the most responsibility
over the longest period; Ellen Jones, Leslie Goodman Perreault,
and Rebecca Slipe were involved at various stages of the project.
Claire Gilchrist, who has been an outstanding secretary and ad-
ministrator for my projects over the past fourteen years, did her
usual wonders with the word processor as we went through successive drafts of the manuscript.

My wife, Beverly, has helped me with all my books, but her
insights and observations were particularly important for this
one. She was a sounding board for my ideas even before they
were committed to paper, and her reactions were invaluable in
my efforts to deal with many complex, emotion-laden issues. My
editor, Michael Aronson, was on the job from the first sentence
to the last; our numerous discussions materially assisted me in
turning a collection of research findings into a book for a general
audience.

Others who read an early rough draft included Perry Beider,
Lawrence Fuchs, Nancy Fuchs-Kreimer, John Kaplan, Seth Krei-
mer, Leslie Goodman Perreault, and Michael Wald. Their
prompt, thoughtful critiques helped me clarify the organization
and structure of the book. Comments on a subsequent draft, gen-
erously provided by Maria Ascher, Gary Becker, Andrew Cherlin,
Sanford Dornbusch, Nannerl Keohane, Frank Levy, and Paul
Milgrom, prompted me to tighten and smooth the exposition. I
am also grateful to Laurie Simon Bagwell, Alan Garber, and
Eleanor Maccoby for advice on particular points. Contributions
from other colleagues are acknowledged with specific references
in the book.

During the course of the research I presented preliminary re-
sults in a variety of settings: a conference titled "The Family and
the Distribution of Economic Rewards," organized by Brigham
Young University; a seminar in the Department of Economics,
Harvard University; and, at Stanford University, meetings at the
Center for Economic Policy Research, the Law School, and the
Center for the Study of Families, Children, and Youth. The dis-

cussions that followed these presentations were always instructive.

I'm also grateful to the Rockefeller Foundation for the opportunity to spend four weeks at the Foundation's Bellagio Study and Conference Center, Lake Como, Italy, in September 1987. The policy chapters were drafted while I was in residence at the center, and I presented my conclusions at a meeting of the foundation's Board of Trustees. The comments received at that meeting and in subsequent private conversations with board members and other Bellagio scholars were most helpful.

No one who is mentioned in these acknowledgments should be held responsible for any shortcomings of the book. The analysis, the interpretations, and the policy recommendations are mine alone, and any errors, alas, are mine also. I expect that some readers will not like my results, but I hope that all will agree with my conclusion that our ability to understand and deal with gender inequality is of vital importance to our nation's future.

Contents

Alfred North Whitehead was asked "Which are more important, facts or ideas?" The philosopher reflected for a while, then said: "Ideas *about* facts."

—Lucien Price,
 *Dialogues of Alfred
 North Whitehead*

Chapter 1

Introduction

The year was 1963. In Washington, Congress passed the Equal
Pay Act. A year later Title VII of the Civil Rights Act would
prohibit all forms of discrimination in employment. In New
York, *The Feminine Mystique* (Friedan 1963) and *Sex and the
Single Girl* (Brown 1962) were becoming best-sellers. All over
the country, women were gaining better control of their fertility
through new methods of contraception such as the Pill and the
IUD. A "sex-role revolution" was under way.

Women's search for political, social, and economic parity with
men did not, of course, begin in the early 1960s. But an unusual
confluence of forces and events, superimposed on long-term economic trends, marked those years as the beginning of a quarter-
century of extraordinary changes in gender roles and relationships. For many women it was a time of great expectations: the
sexes would become equal in the labor market and a new generation of men would become full partners in childcare and housework.

Jump to the late 1980s. A generation has passed and much has
changed. One out of two new mothers returns to a paid job before her baby's first birthday—four times as many as in 1960.
More than one-third of the new lawyers, physicians, and other
doctoral degree recipients are women—up from one in sixteen.
The divorce rate has doubled; so has the proportion of women
not married. Fertility has been below replacement level every year
since 1973, and one out of five new mothers is unmarried.

Amid all this ferment there is another story: the persistence of large differences in gender roles and circumstances. In the labor market, occupational segregation is still widespread, women are much more likely than men to work part time, and they still earn much less for each hour of work. In the home, women continue to provide the bulk of the childcare and other nonmarket work. As one perceptive writer noted after extensive interviews with women in a variety of settings, "It's all so strange . . . I can't believe so little has changed when so much has" (Fleming 1986). Women's goal of economic equality is far from realization.

What is the nature and extent of gender inequality in economic life? Why does it arise? How has it been changing? What are the obstacles to further change? Should public policy be brought to bear on this issue? If so, how? And with what consequences? Frank and reliable answers to these questions are urgently needed by government policymakers, by employers, by judges and educators and counselors, and by millions of women and men who are trying to understand and resolve their own particular version of the "battle of the sexes." To suggest some answers and to help readers develop their own are the principal purposes of this book.

The socioeconomic aspects of the sex-role revolution have certainly not gone unnoticed; indeed, recent years have witnessed a torrent of books, articles, and television programs devoted to gender issues. Why, then, another volume on this subject? My goal is ambitious: to provide a more wide-ranging, more balanced, and especially more analytical treatment of such complex and emotional issues as occupational segregation, the "feminization" of poverty, and equal pay for comparable worth. Thus, this study differs from most previous work in several ways.

First, there seems to be need for a book that not only documents the problems that women face but also probes deeply to discover *why* things are the way they are. Second, although this book is based on detailed empirical research, greater weight is given to providing a framework that will help readers place the quantitative material in context. During the past three years my research assistants and I have pored over scores of statistical volumes and government data tapes on many aspects of gender. My purpose, however, is not only to summarize these statistics but to interpret them, and to present concepts that will assist the reader to make her or his own interpretation. Finally, this book not only discusses policies that might help women but also considers carefully their likely consequences for the entire society.

My most important empirical finding is that the gap between women and men in economic well-being was no smaller in 1986 than in 1960. (Economic well-being depends on money income plus the imputed value of goods and services produced within the household plus leisure as measured by time available after paid and unpaid work.) The women/men ratio of money income almost doubled, but women had less leisure while men had more, an increase in the proportion of adults not married made more women dependent on their own income, and women's share of financial responsibility for children rose. A striking exception is the experience of young, white, unmarried, well-educated women, who made large gains relative to their male counterparts. (These women are mostly single, but divorced and widowed are included.) Most of these women are childless; those who are mothers frequently live under great pressure.

The persistence of substantial gender inequality after a quarter-century of massive social change gives motivation and urgency to the book's other themes. If women were well on their way to economic equality, and if their gains bore no relation to fertility or the care of children, some other subject would command our attention. But the gender gap is still large, and women's efforts to close it are closely related to the low birthrate and to the problems facing young children.

My second important conclusion is that women's inferior economic position and lack of progress since 1960 are not primarily the result of prejudice or exploitation by employers. There is prejudice, and there is exploitation, but the enormous amount of sex segregation by occupation and industry, the huge gap in wages, and the unequal burdens in the home are attributable mostly to other factors. Millions of women believe that they earn less than men because they are women, and they are correct. But that is not the same as saying they earn less because employers discriminate against them.

The book's third critical conclusion is that women's weaker economic position results primarily from conflicts between career and family, conflicts that are stronger for women than for men. More specifically, many different kinds of evidence suggest that *on average* women feel a stronger desire for children than men do and a greater concern for their welfare after they are born. This desire and this concern create an economic disadvantage for women which is strongest at ages 25 to 45, but the effects remain throughout life. Furthermore, I will show why even women who never marry and/or never have children are disadvantaged in the labor market by the same set of forces. Much as some might wish it otherwise, these conclusions are more consistent with the evidence than any others that have been proposed.

My findings provide the background for the policy questions addressed in the last three chapters of the book. The causes and the consequences for society of low fertility are explored, as are several disturbing trends in the well-being of children. I develop the economic arguments in support of policies to help women, and I examine the likely effects of alternative approaches. Labor market policies such as equal pay for work of comparable worth and affirmative action are compared with child-centered policies such as subsidized daycare, parental leaves, and family allowances. The book concludes with sketches of four possible scenarios for the future, along with my personal policy recommendations. The latter are based, as all policy choices must be, on values as well as analysis.

Many of the issues discussed in this book are highly controversial. While seeking to avoid polemics, I do not evade this controversy. In developing my conclusions I have tried to be fair, but not fearful; balanced, but not banal. I have been studying human behavior and social institutions from an economic perspective for more than thirty years, and when I believe that the weight of evidence on a particular question is strongly on one side, I say so rather than sit forever on the fence. On the other hand, when I believe that available theory and data are inadequate to resolve an issue, I do not hesitate to say that either. In short, while hewing to as strict a scientific standard as possible in a book for the general reader, I have tried to be interesting and helpful to a wide audience, including policymakers in the public and private sectors.

When I speak of looking at things from an "economic perspective," what does that mean? First and foremost it means recognizing that we do not live in the Garden of Eden. In the Garden scarcity was unknown, but everywhere else human wants exceed available resources. Thus, the fundamental *economic* problem of every individual and of every society is how to allocate resources so as to best satisfy wants. From this perspective, terms like "free daycare" or "low-cost daycare" are misleading because daycare requires labor, land, and capital that could be used to satisfy some other want; it cannot ever really be free, and good-quality care cannot be low cost. The true social cost of daycare is the value of the forgone alternatives as reflected in the resources used to produce the care.

The economic perspective also sensitizes us to the fact that when people experience a change in their external circumstances they are likely to change their behavior. For instance, a public or private subsidy for daycare will increase the number of parents seeking care for their children, will increase labor force participation, and possibly even increase fertility. Or suppose the government, in order to make daycare more affordable, freezes the prices that daycare centers can charge their clients. The economic perspective leads us to expect an increase in the quantity of care demanded and a decrease in the quantity supplied. Waiting lists will get longer, and various "gray" or "black" markets will probably develop.

The consequences of such a price freeze from an efficiency point of view are relatively unambiguous: it will tend to distort the allocation of resources. The distributional consequences are more difficult to predict. Low-income families may be helped, but that is not certain. If prices are frozen and waiting lists are long, daycare centers may begin to use criteria for admission that hurt some low-income families (for example, requiring parents to participate several times a week). If the price freeze persists, the quality of care is likely to deteriorate because daycare centers will not be able to pay the wages necessary to attract high-quality personnel. Wealthy parents may be able to substitute private caregivers while lower-income parents may not. Among families at the same income level, inequities are likely to increase as the scarce places at daycare centers are allocated on the basis of "connections" and political pull.

Economic theory tells us what shifts in behavior are likely to result from a change in external circumstances; empirical research provides estimates of how large the response is likely to be. Neither theory nor empirical research, however, provides a perfect guide to the future. Sometimes theory suggests multiple effects that work in opposite directions. For example, a general increase in real wages will induce some workers to work more hours (because the "price" of leisure has gone up) and some to work fewer hours (because income has risen and they want to buy more leisure). Whether the price effect or the income effect will dominate is an empirical question, and the answer is likely to vary with the worker's age, sex, marital status, and other characteristics. Even empirical research cannot be definitive because the behavioral response observed in one time or place may not be duplicated in another. Despite these shortcomings, the economic perspective is frequently of great value. To neglect it—to assume that resources are unlimited, or that human behavior is insensitive to changes in prices, wages, taxes, or subsidies—could lead to disastrous policies.

Although the economic perspective is usually necessary for good policymaking, it is not sufficient. A full analysis of the problems of gender, for instance, requires perspectives provided by anthropology, biology, the humanities, law, psychology, sociology, and other disciplines. Contributions from these sources have widened my understanding of the many facets of gender in human society, but this book does not attempt to provide a full-scale multidisciplinary synthesis. I am an economist and I concentrate on the insights that flow from that perspective. It must be emphasized that the explanations and predictions of economics are concerned primarily with the behavior of people in the aggregate, not with individual differences. Why Jane has four children and Sally has none may have nothing whatever to do with economics, but economic factors may be very important in explaining the fall in the U.S. birthrate in the nineteenth century or the baby boom of the 1950s.

A second and even more important caveat regarding policy concerns the role of *values*. Even if economic theory and empirical research were perfect in their predictions, policy choices must be guided by values as well as by analysis. It is one thing to know that if childcare is subsidized certain changes in fertility and labor force participation will follow; whether or not those changes are considered desirable is another matter. At the root of many policy conflicts are deep-seated value differences concerning the nature of the human enterprise and the vision of a good society.

Values not only enter at the point of policy choice, but also may influence the process of research. According to the late Swedish economist Gunnar Myrdal, "Valuations are always with us. Disinterested research there has never been, and can never be. Prior to answers there must be questions. There can be no view except from a viewpoint. In the questions raised and the viewpoints chosen, valuations are implied" (1987, p. 275).

Readers are entitled, therefore, to know something about my background and values. I am a professional economist and have spent most of my adult life as a teacher and researcher. My résumé, however, also includes service as a personnel officer in the Army Air Corps during World War II, a four-year stint as an executive in a small business after the war, and two years on the program staff of a major foundation. These experiences have made me wary of drawing inferences from economic theory alone—I always want to test theories against data and practical experience.

My research agenda has been heavily influenced by the studies

I made of the service economy in the 1960s (Fuchs 1968, 1969). Since then, I have concentrated on applying economics to some of the principal problems of postindustrial society, including health and medical care (1974, 1986a), the family (1983), and gender issues (1971, 1986b).

I am by temperament an optimist, by training a skeptic. Politically I am a liberal both in the nineteenth-century sense of wanting to create maximum opportunity for individuals to pursue their own interests and aspirations, *and* in the twentieth-century sense of wanting to balance the pursuit of freedom with concerns about justice and security. Thus, I reject both centralized control and libertarian approaches in favor of a balanced society that includes significant roles for the market, government, and private institutions such as families, churches, and nonprofit organizations.

I am very much a "family" man, with strong commitments to wife, children, grandchildren, and many others. And I am a religious person, in the sense that the principal function of religion is to inculcate faith in the possibility of human improvement (Kaplan 1957, p. 23).

A final caveat about this book is in order. It may seem to be unduly focused on women. How and why are women changing their behavior? What do women want? What are the problems women face? In my view the gender issues are relevant to both men and women—but interest in them appears to be very unequal. As I pursued research for this book, it became clear that what I was observing was *women's* quest for economic equality—not men's. Most writers report the same impressions. For instance, journalist Anthony Astrachan, in *How Men Feel,* says, "The proportion of all men who genuinely support women's demands for independence and equality is very small. I would guess . . . between five and ten percent" (1986, p. 402). Or, as a leading authority on gender relationships notes, "It is women, by and large, who have been unhappy with the inequitable distribution of roles and work in our culture" (*Healthcare Forum* 1987, p. 27).

To be sure, throughout the ages some men have pressed the case for women's rights. In Germany in 1792 (the same year that Mary Wollstonecraft published her seminal *Vindication of the Rights of Women*), Theodore Gottlieb von Hipple's book *On Improving the Status of Women* appeared. His sympathetic discussion of the disadvantages faced by women and his arguments for their removal had no discernible impact. In the nineteenth century one of England's most influential thinkers, John Stuart Mill, took up the feminist cause in *The Subjection of Women* (1869). This book was the only one by Mill on which his publisher lost money (Sen 1985).

Mill and von Hipple were exceptions. More typical were the views of Leo Tolstoy, who, despite his sympathetic portrayals of women in novels and short stories, wrote in his diary: "To regard them [women] as equals is cruelty" (1891) and "For the existence of a reasonable moral society it is necessary for women to be under the influence of men" (1905).

In my experience in giving academic seminars, talking to lay groups and the press, and in other exchanges, it is usually women, not men, who show most interest in gender issues and who want further change. This is understandable. Many (but not all) of the changes that women have been seeking will impose costs on men. Sometimes the question is literally "His or hers?" Either consciously or subconsciously, men recognize this and resist; one form of resistance is indifference.

But the stakes are much higher than a simple struggle over shares. The decisions that individual women and men make with respect to work, marriage, fertility, and childcare affect their communities, their states, and the nation. A wise public policy will seek to take these effects into account—will seek to make private decisions more consonant with the social good. Despite disappointments, women's quest for equality is likely to persist. To build a strong and vibrant society and an efficient and prosperous economy, Americans will need to find a reasonable way to accommodate that quest.

Chapter 2

The Revolution and Its Roots

The dramatic changes in gender roles, relationships, and expectations of the past quarter-century have often been characterized as a "sexual" revolution. But an increase in awareness and expression of female sexuality is only part of the story; future historians are likely to regard gender-related changes in work and family as having wider and more enduring implications.

Let us look closely at the most important of these changes—the surge of women into paid employment, the fall in fertility, and the decline of marriage—and let us consider their interrelations. Our focus will be on the United States during the last several decades, but it is significant that similar changes have been observed in virtually all industrialized nations. Moreover, in many instances these changes continue trends that have been developing for a century or more. It is the *pace* of recent change, not the direction, that has been most unusual.

What were the roots of the sex-role revolution? In the second part of this chapter we will examine the various explanations that have been offered. We will see that economic, technologic, and demographic changes, along with the women's movement, legislation, and the media, all played a role. We will also see how interactions and feedbacks magnified the effects of the initial stimuli.

Major Changes

Employment

"It is through gainful employment," wrote Simone de Beauvoir, a pioneer of modern feminism, "that woman has traversed most of the distance that separated her from the male; and nothing else can guarantee her liberty in practice" (1949/1961, p. 639). For the past forty years American women have been increasingly acting on that advice: the most persistent change in gender roles since the end of World War II has been the surge of women into paid employment.

Women seek work for many of the same reasons as men: it provides income, fringe benefits, social interactions, a sense of accomplishment, and an answer to the question "What do you do?" The oft-heard explanation, "Women work because they have to," is misleading. Of course the desire to augment the family's income plays a role, but this is because most couples aspire to a higher standard of living. The average husband earned more in *real dollars* in 1987 than in 1960—a year when four out of five married women with young children specialized in housework and childcare. (Since the early 1970s, however, the real wages of men under age 40 have fallen.) Looking to the future, it is unlikely that most married women would give up their paid jobs even if men's earnings were to rise appreciably.

Many women view employment as the passport to full participation in our society, just as the right to own land in Hellenistic Egypt marked a major advance for women in that society (Pomeroy 1984). A Swedish study of working women concluded, "These days women are in the labor force for more reasons than 'just' for the income. Having a job (other than being a housewife) is now regarded as a self-evident right by many women, and it is given the support of Swedish society" (Hoem and Hoem 1986).

Overall trend. In 1960 only 35 percent of women (ages 16 and over) held paid jobs, but by 1986 the proportion had jumped to

51 percent. During this same period the proportion of men with paid jobs fell from 79 to 70 percent. Women's share of persons employed has increased every year since 1947 with the single exception of 1953, when it declined a trivial two-tenths of a percentage point. Starting from a proportion of 28 percent in 1947, it rose to 32 percent in 1957, 36 percent in 1967, 41 in 1977, and 45 in 1987 (see Figure 2.1). On average, women's share rose by almost half a percentage point every year; the pace of change was extremely steady except for slight accelerations during the Korean and Vietnam wars.

Three factors account for the upward trend. The least important is the falling employment rate of men, primarily those 55 or

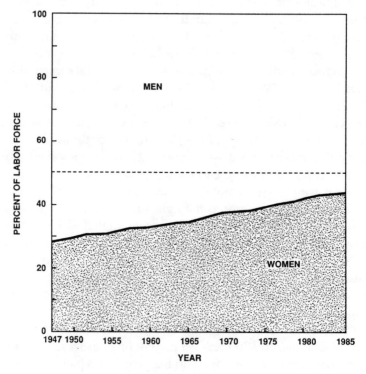

Figure 2.1   Relative shares of persons employed.

older. Second, the employment rate of married women has risen sharply. Most important, the proportion of women not married—a group that has always had relatively high employment—has jumped from 22 to 37 percent at ages 18–64. The rise in the proportion of women who are unmarried has been so large that their share of total female employment actually increased despite the sharp growth in the employment rate of married women.

It has been alleged that women constitute a "reserve" labor force that is called on when the demand for labor is strong and discarded when it is weak, but Figure 2.1 makes it clear that women's share of employment has risen steadily through bad times as well as good. Indeed, in those years when unemployment rose most rapidly (1949, 1954, 1958, 1975, and 1982), women's share of employment actually grew slightly faster than in less troubled years.

Older women lead the way. The steadiness of the overall increase conceals two disparate trends related to age. Older women (45–64) were the first ones to increase substantially their participation in paid work, as can be seen in Figure 2.2. Between 1950 and 1962—that is, prior to antidiscrimination legislation or widespread articulation of feminist aspirations—older women increased their participation rates very rapidly, by about one percentage point per year. After 1963, younger women (25–44) showed big increases, while the rate for older women slowed appreciably. By 1985 participation rates were much higher for the younger women (71 percent) than for those 45–64 (53 percent), whereas in 1960 the rates were 40 and 44 percent, respectively.

Mothers of small children. In relative terms, employment increased most rapidly for married women who have young children (under age 6) at home; in 1960 fewer than one in five were in the labor force, but by 1986 one in two had a paid job. Some of this change is probably a response to the poor economic circumstances facing young husbands after 1973 (Levy 1987), but the influx of young mothers into paid work cannot be explained only by adverse trends in men's income. On average, husbands of employed women with young children earned 29 percent more

in 1986 than in 1960, after adjustment for inflation. Furthermore, employment rates rose faster among women whose husbands had high income—not low—as shown in Figure 2.3.

Higher-level jobs. In 1960 the higher-level professional and
managerial occupations were almost exclusively male preserves.
Only 6 percent of the *new* lawyers, physicians, and doctoral degree recipients were women, whereas 94 percent were men—a
ratio of 16 to 1. By 1985, more than one-third of the new entrants to those high-level jobs were women—the ratio was less
than 2 to 1. The proportions of women *holding* such jobs, however, has changed much less because the big increase in comple-
tion of graduate and professional training has been very recent.
Over two-thirds of the gain has been since 1975. It will take

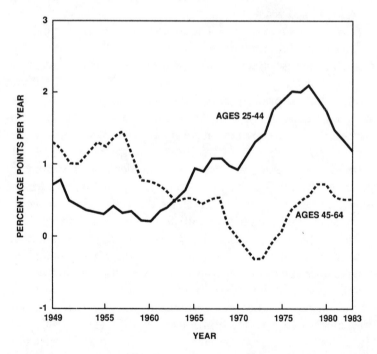

Figure 2.2 Annual change in female labor force participation rate (five-year
moving average).

another generation for the employment statistics to reflect fully recent changes in the willingness and opportunity of young women to prepare themselves for careers requiring large imvestments of time, money, and effort.

Fertility

Americans are not replacing themselves. In 1986 there were only 65 births per 1,000 women ages 15–44, a far lower rate of childbearing than in the worst year of the Great Depression. The decline has been pervasive: women of all races and education and at all ages are having fewer children than they did a generation ago. In 1960 the general fertility rate (births per 1,000 women of childbearing age) was 118, well above the replacement rate of 70. (This rate would yield an average of 2.1 births per woman over thirty years of potential childbearing. Deaths in infancy and

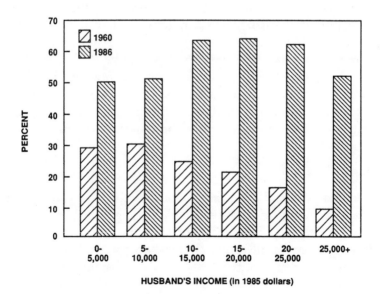

Figure 2.3 Employment rates of married women with child(ren) under six years of age, by husband's income.

childhood would result in two children reaching adulthood, thus just replacing their parents.) The initial declines from this baby boom high were not particularly noteworthy, but by 1973 the rate had fallen below replacement level and it has remained below every year since.

Much of the decline reflects a trend toward smaller families—one or two children instead of three or four; but it also reflects a substantial growth in childlessness. In 1960 only 18 percent of all women ages 25–39 did not have a child in their household. By 1986 the proportion had jumped to 28 percent. Among white women in their late twenties in 1986, more than 40 percent were childless. This may be only a postponement of childbearing, but some demographers believe it presages an increase in the proportion of women who will never give birth (Bloom and Trussell 1984).

Of the babies that are being born, single mothers deliver one in five; a generation ago the proportion was only one in twenty. As is true of the decline in fertility, the increase in the proportion of births out of marriage is evident for women of every socioeconomic status. For blacks the proportion jumped from 24 to 60 percent, and for whites from 2 to 14 percent by 1985. (Throughout this book when blacks are compared with whites, the latter category includes other races such as Asian, who comprise only a few percent of the total and whose earnings, education, and fertility are not significantly different from those of whites.)

Marital Status

Between 1960 and 1986 the proportion of women ages 25–44 who were not married almost doubled, rising from 17 to 31 percent. This reflected increases in the proportion never married and in the proportion divorced. (Widowhood declined somewhat.) The number of unmarried men also rose, but unmarried women in their thirties and forties had fewer prospects for marriage because men tended to marry women younger than themselves.

Never married. Marriage is still the norm for most American adults, but during the past twenty-five years the percent of women who had never married by specific ages has been rising at an unprecedented rate. Figure 2.4 traces out the story in detail, beginning with the cohort of women born in the years 1941–1945. (A cohort consists of people born during the same period of time.) When these women were ages 20–24 (in 1965), only one-third had never been married. Five years later, when they were ages 25–29, only 12 percent were still single. Each successive cohort of women has had a higher percentage who were never married at each age. Of the women born in 1961–1965, well over half (57 percent) were still single in 1985, when they

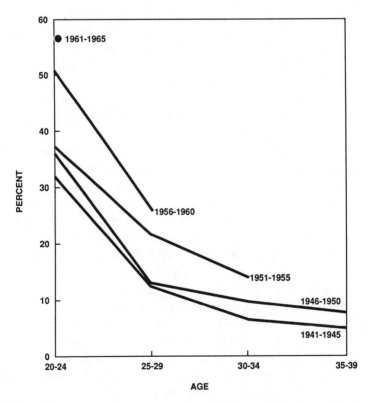

Figure 2.4   Percent of women never married, by age and cohort of birth.

were ages 20–24. This is the highest rate ever experienced in U.S. history. Even the women born in 1916–1920, who came to maturity in the Great Depression, had only 47 percent not married by ages 20–24. Moreover, marriage rates for this cohort soared in the 1940s. By ages 30–34, only 9 percent of the women had never been married.

Divorce. The *never* married contribute to the pool of *not* married, but more than half of the increase in the proportion of women who are unmarried comes from divorce. The percentage of first marriages ending in divorce by given ages has grown rapidly, as shown in Figure 2.5. Unlike the percent never married, however, the most recent cohorts of women (born after 1955) do not show much greater propensity to divorce than those born in 1951–1955. The biggest jump came between the women born in 1941–1945 and those born in 1946–1950. Census Bureau demographers Moorman and Norton (1987) estimate t'.at the latter cohort will eventually have 56 percent of their first marriages ending in divorce, a record high. These are the same women who were in the forefront of the reduction in fertility in the late 1960s and early 1970s.

Although there is clearly some connection between changes in divorce and employment and fertility, the time trend of divorce differs and has a distinctive pattern of its own. During the 1950s and early 1960s, the divorce rate was stable despite rapid increases in the proportion of older women in paid employment. Between 1965 and 1975 the rate quickly doubled, from 10 to 20 divorces per year per thousand married women. It then grew more slowly and reached an all-time high of 22.8 in 1979. Since then the rate has actually declined slightly.

The most likely explanation for this unusual pattern is that many couples experienced *unexpected* changes in circumstances, attitudes, and expectations during the late 1960s and early 1970s. It is an unexpected change that is most disruptive of any relationship, whether employment, partnership, or marriage. Recent changes in sex roles have been more predictable and hence less disruptive. Also, currently many young men and women live together in conjugal unions rather than in legal marriages. These unions have a high rate of dissolution, but are not counted as divorces because the couples were never formally married.

Sex ratio of the unmarried. The rapid increase in the number of never-married and divorced women has provoked considerable discussion regarding their prospects for marriage—prospects that depend heavily on the number of unmarried men. (Differences in the prevalence of homosexuality among men and women also play a role.) The sex ratio, expressed as the number of unmarried men per hundred unmarried women of the same age, declines rapidly over the life cycle, as shown in Figure 2.6. Until

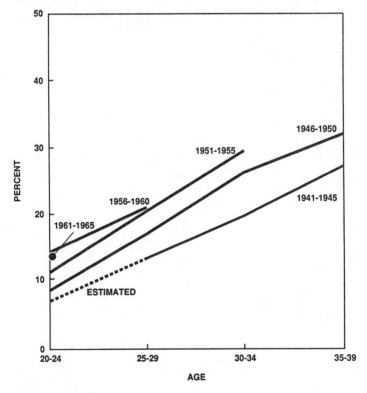

Figure 2.5 Percent of women divorced after first marriage, by age and cohort of birth.

age 35 there are actually more unmarried white men than women, but at ages 35–39 there were only 85 men per hundred women in 1985, and only 58 per hundred at ages 45–49. (Comparisons for blacks are less reliable because many young black men are missing from the Census enumerations and Current Population Surveys that are used to calculate these ratios.)

The sex ratio drops as a cohort ages, for two reasons: mortality rates are higher for men than for women, and older men tend to marry younger women. At ages 35–39 or even 45–49, excess mortality explains only a small part of the man shortage. Most of it arises from selective marrying out of the cohort. For instance, in 1986 at age 35–39 almost half (44 percent) of all married men had a wife in a younger age group, 8 percent had a wife in an

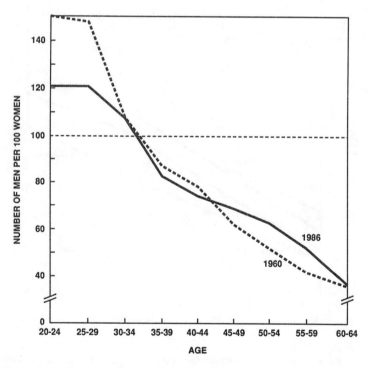

Figure 2.6   Sex ratio of unmarried whites by age.

older age group, and the balance in the same age group. Among men 45–49, more than half (54 percent) of their spouses were in a younger age group.

Given the tendency for men to marry younger women, it is useful to recalculate the sex ratio by comparing the number of unmarried women in an age group with the number of men in the group five years older, as shown in Figure 2.7. We see that for women in their thirties or forties in 1986, the ratio is much below what it was for those ages in 1960 and much below the ratios shown in Figure 2.6. The disparity arises from the uneven size of cohorts born in the 1930s, 1940s, and 1950s. For instance, the number of births in 1941–1945 exceeded the number

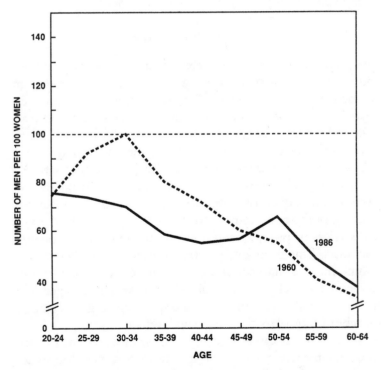

Figure 2.7   Sex ratio of unmarried whites by age (men five years older than women).

in 1936–1940 by 19 percent, and then in 1946–1950 total births were up an additional 24 percent. Those women born while the birthrate was rising rapidly have many fewer potential mates in the cohorts born five years before them.

Figure 2.7 provides a dramatic statistical picture of this "marriage squeeze" that so many women face at mid-life in the 1980s. This is a permanent problem for the women born in the 1940s and 1950s; there will always be fewer men older than themselves. For women in general, however, it is a temporary situation. Indeed, those women born in the 1960s and early 1970s, when total births were falling rapidly, have larger numbers of men older than themselves. It is the men in those cohorts who face a "marriage squeeze."

Reasons for Change

The preceding list of major alterations in the nation's economic and social fabric immediately suggests a number of important and perplexing questions. To what extent are these changes interrelated—part of a "package" in which women's work and marriage and fertility change together in a predictable manner? Is one of the behaviors more fundamental, and the others more derivative? Will these trends continue? Stabilize? Reverse themselves?

Many important, even crucial, decisions depend on the answers to these questions. Business managers require an understanding of these phenomena to determine what kinds of goods and services to produce, and how and where to reach potential customers. Employers in all sectors, private and public, need to rethink their recruitment efforts, their benefit programs, indeed all their personnel policies. Public policymakers have to ponder a wide variety of laws, regulations, and spending programs ranging from birth control to divorce to child welfare.

No single cause can explain all the phenomena over all the decades, but there is widespread agreement that the changes are highly interrelated. The decline in fertility, for instance, has implications for each of the other phenomena. Other things equal, the fewer children a woman has, the more likely she is to work at a paid job. The more likely she is to work, the more incentive she has to invest in the education and training required for higher-level occupations. These factors also contribute to a rise in divorce and to the probability of not marrying at all. Indeed, at least in a statistical sense, the decline in fertility also helps explain the rise in the proportion of births to unmarried women: most of the decline in fertility reflects a trend away from large families (that is, a decline in third-, fourth-, and higher-order births), whereas most of the births to unwed mothers are first or second births.

Another plausible way of describing the cycle of change would start with improved work opportunities for women instead of lower fertility. These opportunities lead them to have fewer children, make them less willing to enter or remain in unsatisfactory marriages, and so on. In principle, one could also start with the rise in the probability of divorce. The prospect of divorce would induce women to have fewer children, to stay more attached to the labor market, and possibly to avoid marriage altogether. Although social scientists are not agreed as to what triggered these cycles of change, the answer can be found in a blend of the following explanations.

Rising Real Wages

Economist Jacob Mincer, in his classic study "Labor Force Participation of Married Women: A Study of Labor Supply" (1962), noted that married women allocate their time among paid work, work at home, and leisure. The "price" of work at home and leisure depends on the market wage. An increase in women's market wage implies an increase in the price of time spent working at home or in leisure, and this price rise leads to a decrease in the quantity demanded (that is, an increase in paid work). The effect will be particularly strong if it is easy for women to use some of their increased earnings to buy goods and services that substitute for the forgone work at home (for example, prepared foods, clothing that needs less care, disposable diapers). This explanation does not require that women's wages increase relative to men's, but simply that they increase in absolute terms. If the wife's wages rise relative to her husband's, there will be a particularly strong incentive for her to increase her share of the couple's total market work.

The wage explanation seems to work well for the 1950s and 1960s, when real wages were rising at a rapid rate and so was the labor force participation of married women. The explanation is less satisfactory for the 1970s and 1980s because real wages stopped growing for women (and men), but the surge of married women into paid work continued as strongly as in the previous decade.

Rising real wages not only brings married women into paid work, but also leads to lower fertility because childcare is particularly *time intensive*. An increase in the value of women's time implies an increase in the price of children. Of course, rising wages mean higher income, but unless the effect of higher income on the demand for children is strong, the higher price of children is likely to lead couples to want smaller families. Economists Gary Becker and Gregg Lewis (1973) have argued that the effect of higher income on demand is likely to be weak because when a couple's income rises, the amount they want to spend on *each child* tends to rise also. Thus, even though total expenditures on children may grow as rapidly as income, most of the growth will be reflected in increased spending per child, not in the number of children per couple. A similar relationship prevails in the automobile market. On average, expenditures for automobiles rise as family income rises, but most of the additional spending is for more expensive cars rather than for a greater number of cars.

The Growth of a Service Economy

The service industries (retail trade, financial services, education, health, personal services, public administration, and the like) have traditionally offered much better employment opportunities for women than have mining, manufacturing, construction, and other branches of the industrial sector. In 1960, for instance, three-fourths of nonfarm female employment was in the service sector, compared with less than half of male employment. Women prefer services for many reasons: there is usually no premium on physical strength, hours of work are frequently more flexible and there are more opportunities for part-time work, and service-sector jobs are more likely to be located in or near residential areas, thus making them more attractive to women who bear large responsibilities for childcare and homemaking even when they also work outside the home. The transformation of the United States into a "service economy" provided tens of millions of new job opportunities for women (Fuchs 1968).

To be sure, part of the growth of service employment must be viewed as a result of the increase in labor force participation of married women rather than its cause. Families with working mothers are more likely to eat out, to send their children to nursery school, and to purchase a wide range of personal and professional services. The interplay between women going to work and the growth of service employment provides a fine example of a *feedback loop* in action. The greater the participation of women in market work, the greater the demand for labor in the service industries; the faster the service sector grows, the greater the opportunity for women to find congenial market work.

Such explanations are sometimes disparaged as "circular," but this criticism is not justified when the initial change (for example, in service employment or in the number of women taking paid jobs) comes from outside the loop. Most of the stimulus to service employment results from output per worker growing more rapidly in agriculture and industry; this shifts the demand for labor from those sectors to services (Fuchs 1968). At the other side of the loop many women enter the labor force for reasons unrelated to the growth of services.

Improvements in Contraception

During the 1960s two new, highly effective contraceptive methods—the Pill and the IUD—were adopted by millions of American women. As women acquired more reliable and more convenient control over fertility, several consequences followed: a reduction in unwanted births, more predictable timing of birth, and a reduction in the risks of pregnancy from premarital and extramarital sex. The direction of effects on family size, women's labor force participation, and marriage is easy to infer, but the magnitudes are more difficult to discern.

Improvement in contraception undoubtedly contributed to the decline in fertility; every fertility survey since the 1960s shows a decrease in *unwanted* births. This decrease, however, accounts for only a minor part of the total decline in fertility; Americans are clearly choosing to have fewer children. One of the currently popular forms of birth control—male sterilization—was readily available in 1960 but seldom utilized. The increased demand for male sterilization is not a response to a technologic change, but evidence of a stronger desire to prevent conceptions. The reasons for this desire must lie elsewhere.

It is also relevant that subgroups of the U.S. population such as native-born white women with native-born parents achieved low fertility a century ago, without access to the new contraceptive technology. Many of these women never married, and those who did had below average fertility. The high rate for the country as a whole at that time resulted from high fertility among the large number of immigrants. In short, lowering the cost of birth control does have some effect on fertility, but a decrease in the demand for children has probably been more important in recent decades.

Changes in Cohort Size

When the birthrate fluctuates widely, as it did between the "birth dearth" of the 1930s and the "baby boom" of the late 1950s, the size of cohorts changes dramatically. Economist Richard Easterlin (1980) has argued that these changes have significant economic and social effects. When the large cohorts enter adulthood, competition among them depresses their wages, raises the cost of housing, and contributes to unemployment. Faced with bleak economic prospects, these cohorts postpone marriage, put off having children, or decide to remain childless; and if they do marry, the wife is more likely to work because the couple needs her income. This explanation is particularly attractive for explaining some of the changes in the late 1970s and early 1980s, when the baby boomers descended on the job and housing markets in full force; it is less satisfactory for explaining the economic and social changes of the 1960s, when the economy was booming and the cohorts of new entrants were much smaller.

Legislation

In the four preceding explanations economic, technologic, or demographic changes motivate the behavioral changes in work, marriage, and fertility. Another kind of explanation looks to new laws as the initial source of the trends under review. Three types of legislation have received particular attention.

First, there are the antidiscrimination laws passed in the early 1960s. By outlawing unequal pay for men and women in the same jobs, and by pressing employers to employ more women, these laws have been regarded by some observers as having major importance, but the evidence is not persuasive. It is easy enough to find particular instances where these laws opened up jobs that were previously closed to women or resulted in a realignment of women's pay scales, but it is difficult to see any major effects on broad trends in women's wages or employment. The Equal Pay laws were passed in 1963 and 1964, but fifteen years later the women/men wage ratio was unchanged at about 60 percent. It was only in the 1980s that the ratio started to climb, but these were the "Reagan years"—a period not noted for vigorous enforcement of antidiscrimination and affirmative action legislation. With regard to women's employment, the rate of increase prior to the legislation was as rapid as after the laws were passed.

A second set of laws created new transfer programs such as Aid to Families with Dependent Children, food stamps, and Medicaid. These programs clearly made it more feasible for a woman to raise a family outside marriage, and thus might have contributed to the rise in divorce and the increased proportion of births to unwed mothers. Just as clearly, however, these laws are not likely to have stimulated the growth of female employment or induced the decline in fertility. Moreover, the surge in divorce rates and the postponement of marriage were widespread throughout all socioeconomic groups. It is, therefore, difficult to believe that legislation that affected primarily the poor can stand as a major explanation for widespread social change.

Finally, there were legal changes aimed directly at the family: the legalization and subsidization of abortion and the relaxation of requirements for divorce provide two notable examples. In recent years American women have had about 3.6 million children annually, almost 3 million fewer than they would have had if they were bearing children at the 1960 rate. The abortion rate is now about 1.5 million per year. Even if we assume that every abortion represents an averted birth, abortions would, at most, account for half of the decline in fertility. But that is too high an estimate because the assumption is unreasonable. The experience of countries that have banned abortion (for example, Romania) indicates that women have other ways of averting births, such as increased use of contraception, decreased sexual activity, and illegal abortions. When Romania outlawed abortions, the increase in fertility was much less than the decrease in legal abortions. Thus, the legalization of abortion cannot be the major explanation for the decline in fertility.

The effects of no-fault divorce legislation on marriage are especially difficult to measure. On the one hand, it is easy to see that those couples who are already married would be more likely to remain so if divorce were more difficult to obtain. On the other hand, the ease of divorce may have persuaded some couples to try marriage; if divorce were not easy the marriage rate might be lower than it is. On balance, the former effect is probably stronger, but probably not so strong as to warrant crediting this legislation with a primary role in the changes in marriage, fertility, and work.

In summary, legislation matters, but it is doubtful that it should be assigned a primary explanatory role. To a considerable extent legislators are attuned to the basic socioeconomic forces that reshape individual behavior and they are responsive to the legislative demands posed by the new behaviors. Judicial interpretation of laws is similarly affected. In the words of Mr. Dooley, the voice of political humorist Finley Peter Dunne, "th' Supreme Coort follows th' election returns" (Bander 1901/1981).

Changes in Ideology and Preferences

All of the preceding explanations rely on a change in *external* circumstances to induce a change in behavior, even though underlying preferences remain unchanged. For instance, when divorce becomes easier and less expensive, more couples divorce, even though there may be no change in the number of unhappy marriages and no change in attitudes toward divorce. The change in behavior is as predictable as an increase in air travel if the price of airplane tickets falls. By contrast, some observers believe that recent trends in work, marriage, and fertility are the result of fundamental shifts in preferences or attitudes—that is, shifts that are *internal* to women (and possibly men as well). According to this view, behavioral change originates inside women's heads rather than in the external incentives and constraints that they face.

Economic analysis usually assumes that preferences are fixed and thus focuses on the effects of changes in prices, wages, and income. This approach has a great deal of power, but I believe that it is incomplete; *ideas* expressed in books, articles, and television programs also affect behavior by changing preferences. The media may not provide the initial stimulus, but they amplify it by helping people internalize their responses to economic, technologic, and demographic factors.

An example may help show the relation between the media and changes in external constraints. Suppose, for instance, that a rise in real wages or the growth of a service economy alters the trade-offs that women face between working in the market or staying home and having children. This will pull some women into the labor market and prompt others to think about making a change. It is also likely to provoke a flood of articles, books, newspaper stories, and television programs that rationalize the new behavior. This response by the media requires neither venality on the part of writers nor collusion among publishers. At any given time there are thousands of manuscripts waiting to be published or produced and numerous media competing for the public's attention. Just as with goods and services, there is a *market for messages*. Competition among publishers and television stations forces them to deliver the messages that people want to hear. Why do people want to hear messages that reinforce the changes in behavior that they have undertaken or are considering? Psychologists answer this question in the following way.

When a person has to make a difficult decision, such as a new mother deciding to return to work or a woman deciding not to have children, she may experience a tension between actions and beliefs. Psychologists call this *cognitive dissonance* (Festinger 1957). The tension can be relieved by finding reasons that support the choice made and that denigrate the alternative. For economists the change in external circumstances (e.g., a change in wages or prices) is reason enough for the change in behavior, but most people need other justifications, for themselves as well as for those whose opinions matter to them. The resolution of the dissonance requires that the person actually believe the other justifications. But such belief amounts to a change in preferences. One implication of this sequence of events is that the ultimate change in behavior is likely to be much larger than would be predicted from considering only the effect of the change in external circumstances and ignoring the change in preferences.

Thus, even if ideological forces were not the primary cause of the sex-role revolution, they undoubtedly influenced the behavior of millions of women by making them aware of a wider set of options, by providing a new vocabulary, and by stimulating women to rethink their goals, their roles, and their relationships with other women and men. One of the more striking changes that I have observed during the past quarter-century is the increased appreciation of women for other women—as political leaders, supervisors, colleagues, and friends. Some of this heightened sense of mutual respect comes from objective changes in circumstances such as better job opportunities and better birth control, but the articulation of new ideologies causes more rapid and more widespread diffusion of new attitudes and behaviors.

Conclusion

The most fundamental changes of recent decades were the massive entry of married women into paid work and the steep decline in fertility. The other changes—in marriage and divorce, in training for higher-level occupations, and in childbearing outside marriage—mostly derive from choices about work and fertility. For many women this is a joint decision, expressed as "I will take a paid job *and* have fewer children." In the post–World War II era, the work decision appears to have come first; the increase in married women's employment began in the 1950s, a decade before the decrease in fertility. On the other hand, over the span of a century or more, the fertility decline tended to precede the increase in women's participation in paid work.

Of the many explanations offered for the changes in work and fertility, no single one is completely satisfactory. Some are more convincing for one behavior than for another; some are more consonant with the evidence in the 1950s and 1960s, whereas others are more plausible for the 1970s and 1980s. The growth of employment opportunities in service industries is the factor most consistently present over the entire period, but the changes in behavior are much greater in magnitude than one would expect from this or any other explanation taken alone. I conclude that a combination of factors coincided to induce changes of revolutionary proportions. The initial stimuli were probably economic, technologic, and demographic, but they induced changes in legislation and in the media that affected attitudes and preferences. They also set in motion feedback loops among the interrelated behaviors, and the cumulative effect was a social revolution.

Chapter 3

The More Things Change . . .

The French have a saying, "Plus ça change, plus c'est la même chose"—"The more things change, the more they stay the same." The saying captures the insight that some things are very difficult to change, and that apparent change often conceals actual permanence. It is particularly applicable to women's quest for economic equality because many of the most relevant variables have been remarkably stable despite the trends described in the preceding chapter. Here we will look at those aspects of the labor market that have been particularly resistant to change—occupational segregation, hours of work, the sex gap in wages—and will examine the reasons for their persistence.

Occupational Segregation

The division of labor by sex appears to have been universal throughout human history (Mead 1952, Hartmann 1976, Brown 1986), but it has taken different forms at different stages of economic development. In hunting-and-gathering societies both men and women work to feed and clothe themselves and their children, but their activities are usually gender-specific (Murdock and Provost 1973). In industrial societies like the one that emerged in the United States between 1850 and 1950, the chief difference in sex roles was between market work (mostly men) and work in the home (mostly women).

With the influx of women into paid jobs, this distinction between men and women has become much weaker, but segregation of jobs by sex continues at a very high level. The facts are beyond dispute; the explanations are highly controversial. Some observers believe employers are the main culprits, others blame male workers and consumers, while still others attribute segregation to sex-role differentiation which may be biological or social in origin.

Measurement

There are many measures of occupational sex segregation, but they all show high and only slowly changing levels. One simple, widely used measure, the Duncan index, is calculated by summing the absolute differences between the percent of all men and percent of all women in different occupations and dividing by two. For example, suppose there are three occupations.

	Percent of men	Percent of women	Absolute difference
Occupation A	50	10	40
Occupation B	30	25	5
Occupation C	20	65	45
	100	100	90

The Duncan index in this case would equal $90 \div 2 = 45$ percent.

The Duncan index shows the percent of women (or the percent of men) that would have to change occupations in order to eliminate sex differences in the distributions. A score of 100 percent indicates complete segregation, while a score of zero indicates that men and women have the same relative distributions across occupations. In comparisons limited to year-round full-time wage and salary workers (to eliminate differences that might arise from part-time work and self-employment), the women-men index across 503 occupations was 57 percent in 1980. This means that more than half of all women (men) workers would have to change occupations in order for them to have the same distribution as men (women).

The pervasiveness of occupational segregation by sex comes into sharp perspective when compared with segregation by race. In 1980 the sex segregation index was 57 percent for white women versus white men and for black women versus black men, but the race segregation indexes were only 28 percent for white women versus black women, and 33 percent for white men versus black men (see Table 3.1). When indexes are calculated across industries, segregation by sex (within each race) is almost as great as among occupations and almost twice as pronounced as segregation by race (within each sex). These results are especially remarkable because whites have more education than blacks (women and men have about the same) and racial segregation persists in housing and schooling.

Comparisons of segregation indexes in 1980 with similar indexes for 1960 ("similar" because in the 1960 Census there were only 291 occupations, classified somewhat differently) reveal

Table 3.1. Duncan indexes of occupational segregation by sex and race.

	1960	1980	Change from 1960 to 1980
Women : men			
White	62	57	−5
Black	71	57	−14
Age 25–34	67	55	−12
35–44	63	58	−5
45–54	63	60	−3
55–64	65	61	−4
Education ≤ no high school	66	60	−6
some high school	64	61	−3
high school	66	62	−4
college degree	66	50	−16
graduate degree	56	43	−13
White : black			
Women	56	28	−28
Men	50	33	−17

considerable persistence in segregation by sex among whites, despite the sex-role revolution of the 1960s and 1970s. This stability is in sharp contrast to the trend in segregation by race, which declined sharply between 1960 and 1980. The sex segregation indexes were especially stable at older ages and at lower levels of education. Younger women and better-educated women achieved significant gains in the integration of occupations, but even for these groups segregation by sex is substantially larger than segregation by race. (No samples comparable in size to the Census one-in-one-hundred tapes are available beyond 1980, but analysis of Current Population Survey data for 1986 suggests that there were some relatively small reductions in sex segregation in the 1980s.)

Explanations

Prejudice and exploitation. Why is there so much segregation by sex? Many writers have argued that employers are primarily responsible, because of prejudice or a desire to exploit women workers. When segregation is the result of employer prejudice, profits are lowered because employers deprive themselves of the opportunity to match jobs with the workers best qualified for them. When employers segregate in order to exploit, prejudice is not the issue; the search for profits is. According to this theory, employers discriminate between men and women in job assignments in order to drive down the wages of women and thus make above-normal profits on their labor.

Both versions have some plausibility. I have seen a senior officer of a major corporation launch an emotional tirade at the thought of women entering the executive suite, and I have seen the chief of surgery at a leading hospital get red in the face at the suggestion that women might make capable colleagues. Exploitation is most likely to occur in the proverbial "one-company town" where a single employer may be able to manipulate the demand for labor to take advantage of the limited alternative opportunities available to his work force.

Neither explanation, however, is persuasive for the broad sweep of American industries and communities. Prejudice of employers against women no doubt exists, but prejudice against blacks is at least as prevalent. If employer prejudice were the main cause of occupational segregation, the indexes by race would not be so much lower than those by sex. (Prejudice in schools, churches, housing, and other institutions also contributes to segregation, but again it is difficult to make a case that blacks encounter a great deal less prejudice than women in these areas.) The pattern of sex segregation by educational level also argues against this explanation. If the prejudice of male employers were the principal cause of sex segregation, it should be most evident for workers with high levels of schooling, because then women would be intruding on the employer's own domain. In fact, the Duncan index is much lower for workers with college or graduate degrees than for those with less schooling. By contrast, the segregation index for black men versus white men increases from 27 percent for those with less than a high school education to 34 percent for college graduates and 32 percent for those with graduate degrees.

The exploitation argument also founders on a number of fronts, both theoretical and empirical. For instance, the widespread sex segregation by *industry* that we observe can hardly serve the interests of profit-seeking employers. It is one thing to segregate by occupation in order to drive down women's wages, but employers in the steel industry (90 percent male), for instance, can hardly benefit from pushing women workers into apparel manufacturing (80 percent female). Approximately equal numbers of women and men work in retailing, but some branches (such as auto dealers and gasoline stations) employ mostly men, while others (apparel stores, florists) employ mostly women. It is absurd to suggest that this segregation results from attempts at exploitation of women by owners of gasoline stations.

If exploitation were the explanation for occupational segregation, it ought to be less evident among employers having the least power to exploit. Thus, we should not observe much segregation in highly competitive industries such as retailing or clothing manufacturing—but we do. Also, if the purpose of segregation is to increase profits, those firms and industries with the most segregation ought to be the most profitable (other things equal), but no such pattern has been observed. Finally, the segregation-exploitation explanation is most plausible for small towns where workers have fewer alternative job opportunities. When the analysis is limited to workers in the largest urban areas (population 2 million or more), however, the Duncan index is 55 percent—almost as high as for all workers regardless of location.

Two other pieces of evidence on occupational segregation by sex are particularly noteworthy. First, many observers believe that the government discriminates less than private employers (the wage gap between women and men is smaller in the public sector), but sex segregation in the public sector is as large as among private employees (Jacobsen 1987). Second, segregation is not concentrated in the older, more stagnant industries. When I divided the economy into three sectors according to the rate of growth of employment between 1960 and 1980, the Duncan index for segregation by sex was as large for the industries with rapid growth as for those with average or below average growth.

There are undoubtedly prejudiced and exploitative employers, but I conclude that most of the pervasive sex segregation in the U.S. economy results from other factors. Some segregation is attributable to prejudice by workers or customers, but it is impossible to say how much. Male workers have often resisted the introduction of women into their jobs or workplaces, and there are also cases in which the workers' wives have objected to integration. For some jobs, such as waiting on tables in fine restaurants, it may be the prejudice of customers that inhibits desegregation. Unlike employers whose indulgence of prejudice is often tempered by the pressures of competition, workers and customers are not driven out of the market if they discriminate against women, although they may lose in other ways.

The explanations that focus on employers, workers, or customers assume that women and men are the same, but are perceived or treated differently. Another set of explanations says that segregation results from real differences between women and men, differences that are biological or social in origin.

Biology. The most obvious biological difference between women and men is that women get pregnant, deliver babies, and nurse them; men don't. If fertility were very high and life expectancy low, childbearing would significantly affect the amount and kind of work that women do. But in an era such as the present, when most women have two children or less, and when there are several decades of work possible after the birth of the last child, childbearing *per se* would not be as important except insofar as it leads to enhanced concern about children after birth.

There are other biological differences. On average, men are bigger than women and have more upper body strength (but some women are bigger and stronger than some men). A review of the division of labor by sex in 185 societies in all parts of the world (Murdock and Provost 1973) reveals widespread segregation, much of which appears to be biologically determined. Activities that are exclusively or preponderantly male usually require considerable physical strength, and may require long absences from home. Examples include metalworking, weapon making, hunting, mining, and lumbering. Some predominantly male activities are not so easily explained. The manufacture of musical instruments, for instance, does not always require great strength, but it is exclusively a male activity in eighty-three societies and a female activity in only one. Predominantly female activities include cooking, carrying of water, and preparation of vegetal foods. Murdock and Provost agree with Judith Brown's (1970) conclusion that women's activities are typically compatible with childcare responsibilities (Murdock and Provost 1973, p. 211).

Whatever the importance of size and strength in preindustrial societies, however, these characteristics have little relevance for most occupations in a modern service economy. If the physical demands of work were a major explanation for occupational segregation in the United States, we would expect the index to be higher in the goods sector (which includes manufacturing, mining, construction) than in the service sector (with industries such as retailing, health, and education). In fact, the Duncan indexes are the same in the two sectors. In the steel industry, physical factors may explain why production workers are men and secretaries are women, but the high level of segregation in services must arise primarily for reasons other then gender differences in size and strength.

Besides biological differences in physical size and in the reproduction process, there may be others related to hormones or to sex-related patterns of development. These differences would refer only to averages, however, and there are undoubtedly significant overlaps between women and men in biologically determined distributions of aptitudes, interests, and temperaments. The concept of *overlapping distributions* is particularly relevant to the issue of gender inequality. We are often told that men and women differ with respect to some characteristic: "men are more analytical, women are more intuitive"; "women are more nurturing than men"; "men are more aggressive than women." Taken literally, these statements must be wrong. The most that they can mean is that, *on average,* men are more analytical or women are more intuitive. With respect to any characteristic there is a distribution of men around their average and a distribution of women around theirs, and these distributions overlap. Thus, some women are more analytical than some men, and some men are more intuitive than some women. Height provides a clear example of this phenomenon. In the United States men are, on average, five inches taller than women, but the distributions overlap. For instance, 14 percent of men are shorter than sixty-five inches while 17 percent of women are above that height. Our understanding of many complex gender issues will be enhanced by using the concept of overlapping distributions.

Even if there are differences in averages between women and men with respect to certain characteristics, it seems unlikely that they would be as large as the sex differences observed in the labor market. However, psychologist Richard J. Herrnstein has argued that "minor sex differences in broad averages can translate into major differences in occupational patterns" (1985, p. 180). He notes that if a job has five qualifications, each of which can be met by 60 percent of men and 40 percent of women, an unbiased employer who rejects any applicant who fails to meet one or more of the qualifications, would end up with a labor force that is eight to one male (because $.6^5$ is almost eight times $.4^5$).

The problem with this argument is that it holds only if there is complete independence among all the different qualifications. By contrast, if the presence or absence of qualifications were perfectly correlated across individuals, an unbiased employer would hire 60 percent men and 40 percent women. Complete independence among the qualifications is highly unlikely (for example, willingness to work long hours would probably be associated with willingness to travel), and these associations would substantially reduce the eight-to-one ratio.

Although Herrnstein's analysis is questionable, there are other reasons why relatively small sex differences could lead to large differences in labor market outcomes. Suppose, for instance, that it is very expensive to test individuals to determine their qualifications for a particular job. In that case an employer might simply look at gender and hire only men if they were, *on average,* more likely to be qualified. From the employer's perspective this is a rational choice, not prejudice and not exploitation. Given the average difference, men have a higher probability of being qualified. From the perspective of a qualified woman, however, it is blatant discrimination. Note that women and men whose qualifications are below the average of their group tend to benefit from decisions based on group averages. When the true qualifications of individuals are difficult to discern, this *statistical discrimination* (Phelps 1972) can produce large differentials in hiring, even though there is considerable overlap in the distributions of qualifications among men and women.

Socialization. Not all differences between women and men should be attributed to biology. From infancy onward, girls and boys are socialized differently—by families, schools, churches, and the media—and this socialization significantly affects their behavior as adult women and men. The biological process of childbearing may provide the initial impetus for differentiation, but socialization magnifies its effect. Historically, one of the primary objectives of socialization has been to direct women to the roles of wife, mother, and homemaker, and to direct men to the roles of husband, father, and provider. Not surprisingly, the jobs women take are more likely to be located in residential areas, more likely to afford opportunities for part-time work, and in general to be more compatible with the traditional primary roles.

Socialization can affect occupational segregation through the choice of subjects in school, the pattern of extracurricular activities, and the goals one sets with respect to family, career, friendships, and so on. If, from infancy on, boys and girls are exposed to different circumstances, influences, training, and role models, it should come as no surprise that they reach the labor market with different aspirations, aptitudes, networks, and commitments.

Some socialization seems to promote role differentiation for its own sake. For instance, Murdock and Provost's review of segregation in tribal societies identifies many activities that are reserved to men in some societies and to women in others, but are rarely performed by both sexes in the same society. Examples include the preparation of skins and manufacture of leather products, loom weaving and the making of nets and mats, the preservation of meat and fish, and the preparation of drinks. Margaret Mead noted that "in a great number of human societies men's sureness of their sex role is tied up with their right, or ability, to practice some activity that women are not allowed to practice" (1952, p. 159).

Sex-role differentiation is not a creation of the modern era; indeed, it was probably more pronounced in many earlier societies. There may be economic advantages to this differentiation if there are no good screening mechanisms for assigning young people to training and work on the basis of individual aptitudes and interests. In the absence of formal education, examinations,

and the like, it may be relatively efficient to assign adult roles on
the basis of sex so that all girls and boys know from early childhood what will be expected of them. (This is not a normative
judgment that efficiency considerations ought to outweigh those
of equity, but a positive analysis as to why gender differentiation
might arise and persist in some societies.) Moreover, sex-role differentiation in preindustrial societies is often part of a complex
family or clan system, with numerous rights and obligations dependent not only on gender but on age, marital status, and birth
order. In a world governed by status rather than by individual
contracts or arrangements, gender is usually a significant part of
one's status. In the United States the distinction between an aunt
and an uncle or between a son-in-law and a daughter-in-law may
be small, but in many societies the difference in roles is enormous.

Even in modern societies gender segregation among children
is surprisingly widespread and difficult to explain. Psychologists
Eleanor Maccoby and Carol Jacklin have concluded that the preference of preschoolers for same-sex playmates is unrelated to the
characteristics of the individual child (how masculine or feminine) or whether their parents encourage or discourage cross-
gender interactions. They suggest that there is an internal dynamic to segregation that arises out of "the simple fact that a
child is, and is known to be, a boy or a girl" (1987, p. 283).

Differentiation, however, need not be equated with dominance
of one sex over the other. Peggy Sanday's (1981) survey of studies of more than 150 societies shows that the relative power of
women and men varies greatly from one society to another and
depends upon a wide variety of symbolic, cultural, and economic
factors.

What determines patterns of socialization? One way to think
of the process is from a Darwinian perspective. Different societies
develop different patterns, and some work better than others. A
society with a socialization pattern that is not well suited to the
society's circumstances will tend to disappear or remain small.
Societies with socialization patterns that are highly functional

will tend to flourish and the patterns will tend to spread. Circumstances change, however, and societies need to adapt to those changes. A pattern that worked well when fertility and infant mortality were high and the economy was agricultural or industrial may not work as well for a postindustrial society. Some of the tensions and trauma of the past quarter-century with respect to gender probably reflect the conflict between traditional gender stereotypes and the new circumstances of controlled fertility, longer life span, and a predominantly service economy.

Under current conditions in the United States, socialization for the roles of wife and mother can frustrate women's quest for economic equality in at least two ways. First, it affects the choices women make in school and in the labor market, choices that limit their lifetime earning power. Not infrequently, women who have sacrificed market skills and ambitions in favor of home responsibilities find themselves at a severe economic disadvantage later in life as a result of divorce. Second, even when individual women resist socialization, they are likely to encounter difficulties in the labor market simply because they are women and are often evaluated and treated according to gender norms.

It is important to note that socialization affects the behavior of both sexes. Just as women have been socialized for their roles, men have been socialized for theirs. In fact, socialization is in some ways more important for men than women because motherhood is partly a biologically given role whereas "fatherhood is a social invention" (Mead 1952, p. 183). Some aspects of fatherhood that are most highly valued in contemporary society—such as long-lasting commitment to wife and children—are virtually unknown among the species that are closest to us in nature, for example, chimpanzees and gorillas.

Is socialization more important than biology? That's difficult to say, partly because we don't have data adequate to provide definitive tests and partly because the two explanations interact with each other in a variety of complex ways. Suppose, for instance, that there are some small biological differences between men and women in their preferences for childcare. The effect of these differences on behavior could be magnified by socialization, by statistical discrimination, and by the advantages obtained from specialization and division of labor.

In a similar way, socialization and prejudice are interrelated. A relatively small amount of employer prejudice could be amplified by prejudice in other areas, a prejudice which is virtually indistinguishable from socialization. Economists Francine Blau and Marianne Ferber have noted that "even a relatively small amount of initial labor market discrimination can have greatly magnified effects if it discourages women from making human capital investments, weakens their attachments to the labor force, and provides economic incentives for the family to place priority on the husband's career" (1986, p. 261).

All the explanations have some validity. Employer prejudice undoubtedly exists, but is probably not the primary reason for widespread occupational segregation by sex. Biological differences exist, and were probably the chief explanation at certain stages of economic development. Now socialization is also a major force.

Hours of Paid Work

Women are much more likely to work at a paid job now than they were a generation ago, but the proportion of employed women who work part time has shown no tendency to decline. In 1986, among those women ages 25–64 who were working in the week of the Current Population Survey, more than 20 percent worked fewer than thirty hours. Among men, only 7 percent were in that situation. Furthermore, of those women who had worked thirty hours or more in the survey week, 13 percent had worked fewer than forty weeks in the previous year. Thus, even among employed women of prime working age, one in three work substantially less than a full week or a full year. If "full time" were defined by a more stringent standard, such as a minimum of thirty-five hours per week and at least forty-eight weeks per year, one-half of all employed women would be considered "part-timers."

Which women work part time? Not surprisingly, it is those who are married and those who have a small child at home (see Table 3.2). A husband's presence usually makes part-time work more feasible (less need for full-time income) and increases the demand for her nonmarket work. Marital status has a much smaller effect on the propensity to work part time among black women than white, at least in part because black husbands earn less than white. Among white workers, the proportion working part time is 13 percentage points higher for married than for unmarried women, but among blacks the differential is only 2 percentage points.

The presence of a young child substantially increases the demand for work in the home, making it more difficult to pursue full-time employment. As Sara Davidson, a 1960s radical feminist and 1980s mother, says, "How to reconcile family and career is the crucial unresolved issue in women's lives" (1984, p. 54). Part-time work often provides a compromise solution. Statistical analysis of working women shows that even after controlling for age, education, and similar factors, the presence of a young child increases a woman's probability of working part time by about ten percentage points.

The fact that white married women are much more likely to work part-time than black married women shows that part-time status usually reflects women's choices (given their circumstances) rather than an inability to find full-time work. This infer-

Table 3.2. Percent of employed, ages 25–64, working less than thirty hours per week.

	1960	1986
Men	5	7
Women	19	21
Married	22	25
Not married	10	13
With child under 6	29	29
No child under 6	17	19

ence is confirmed by Bureau of the Census surveys of part-time workers. Women usually cite the need to work at home as the main reason for their working less than full time in the market; men are more likely to say they have difficulty finding a full-time job. There are undoubtedly some women with part-time jobs who would like to work longer hours, but there are probably many more who work full time even though they would prefer fewer hours if they could keep the same job and its associated fringe benefits.

A "natural experiment" by a large manufacturing company in 1985 provided strong evidence on this point. Faced with a fall in demand, the company required all its workers to reduce hours and earnings by 10 percent for six months as an alternative to layoffs. My research assistant and I surveyed over 1,500 of the employees to find out how they felt about the program and how they used the additional time off (Fuchs and Jacobsen 1986). Holding constant age, education, type of job, and many other characteristics, married women were much more likely than married men to favor the program. The difference of 16 percentage points was highly significant in both statistical and practical terms. When children were present, women used most of the time off for housework and childcare and very little for leisure, but men's time use was much less affected by the presence of children.

The propensity for women to work part time is just as prevalent among those with considerable education as among those with less schooling. In 1986 there were more than half a million white women with eighteen or more years of schooling who had at least one child under age 12. Those who were married (87 percent of the total) worked only a little more than half as many hours in the labor market as their husbands (1,246 versus 2,272). (The averages refer to all wives and husbands, including those with zero hours of paid work.) Those women who were not married had an average of 1,751 hours of paid work.

A 1986 survey of the women who had graduated from Wellesley College in 1966 revealed that among those with paid jobs, fully one-third worked part time. Moreover, about a third of those who were working full time said they would prefer part-time employment. Three out of four of the Wellesley alumnae had advanced degrees and virtually all had done some graduate study.

Is women's propensity to work part time a temporary phenomenon—one that is likely to fade in the decades ahead? The evidence from Sweden suggests that it may not be. Sweden has gone much further than the United States in designing private and public policies to promote economic equality between women and men. Employment rates of Swedish women are higher than in the United States, their wages are much closer to men's, and childcare allowances are more generous; nevertheless, a large proportion of Swedish women work part time. The female/male ratio of part-timers is almost six to one in Sweden, much higher than in the United States (Kahne 1985, p. xiii).

Another glimpse into the future comes from a survey I have taken among hundreds of undergraduates at Stanford University during recent years. Both women and men say that happy marriages and successful careers are very important in their vision of a good life. Women give slightly more weight to marriage than men do, but the difference is small, and women attach just as much importance to careers as men do. However, when asked what changes they would make in their paid employment if they had young children, more than 60 percent of the women but less than 10 percent of the men say they would substantially reduce their hours of work or quit work entirely for several years. The adverse effect of this withdrawal on occupational choice and financial success in the labor market is obvious. When queried about the results, the women explain that they define "successful career" differently from the men—with more emphasis on personal satisfaction than on making money or achieving power.

Not only are women more likely to work part time, but even those who have full-time jobs are much less likely than men to work more than 40 hours per week. Among white married women with eighteen years or more of schooling and at least one child under twelve at home, only *one in ten* works more than 2,250 hours per year. By contrast, *half* of their husbands do, and one-third of the men work more than 2,500 hours.

Philadelphia's 30th Street train station provides a vivid example of gender differences at work. Every weekday at about 7:30 A.M. there are hundreds of passengers lining up to board an Amtrak Metroliner for Washington, D.C., or one for New York City. They are mostly in their thirties or forties, well dressed, prosperous. Only a few carry suitcases or overnight bags; most have briefcases or small attaché cases, and many will be returning to Philadelphia that same night after a twelve-hour day. The sex ratio speaks volumes: about four men for every woman.

The desire (or need) for women to work only part time contributes to sex segregation because occupations differ considerably in the opportunities they afford for part-time work (for example, tending a furnace in a steel mill versus selling in a retail store). The higher the proportion of women in any occupation, the higher the proportion of *men* as well as women who work part time. Also, the more male-dominated the occupation, the higher the proportion of *women* as well as men who work long hours. But even holding the sex-mix of the occupation constant, there is a huge sex difference in patterns of work (see Table 3.3). The constraints women face on hours of paid work contribute to the sex differential in wages.

Table 3.3. Part-time and overtime work, nonfarm employed, ages 25 and over, 1980.

Percent of occupation female	Percent usual hours under 30		Percent usual hours over 40	
	Women	Men	Women	Men
0–19.9	12.5	4.6	17.5	33.3
20–39.9	14.9	5.5	16.4	37.8
40–59.9	16.8	6.4	12.3	29.5
60–79.9	25.3	9.0	8.6	24.8
80–100.0	23.8	11.8	6.8	20.2

The Wage Gap

Throughout history, women have earned less than men. Cleopatra was the absolute ruler of Egypt, but men's wages were more than double those of women in Egyptian workshops and manufacturies during her reign (Pomeroy 1984). According to economic historian Claudia Goldin (1986), American women working in manufacturing in 1820 earned only 35 percent as much as their male counterparts; and in mid-nineteenth century England, male spinners were paid more than twice as much as female powerloom weavers (Tannahill 1980).

Between 1890 and 1930 the female/male wage ratio in the United States jumped from about .45 to .60 and then remained at about that level for half a century. After 1979 women's wages began to rise relative to men's, but even in the mid-1980s the average American woman earned only two-thirds as much as the average man for each hour of work. This wage gap is the most obvious and the most important evidence of economic inequality; many feminist leaders have set its elimination or substantial reduction as a primary goal.

Facts about the Wage Gap

White women earn much less than white men per hour of work; among blacks the sex gap in wages is smaller, although still substantial. The ratios in Table 3.4 cover all nonfarm employed persons who worked at least thirty hours per week. The first column is based on actual earnings; the second shows the earnings ratios adjusted for differences in the average years of schooling of the two groups under comparison. This adjustment raises the women/men ratio slightly for whites because employed men have, on average, slightly more education than employed women, but it lowers the ratio for blacks because the sex differential in education is reversed.

We have seen that occupational segregation by sex is much greater than by race; the enormous sex difference in earnings also becomes more vivid when compared with the race differential. Despite centuries of racial discrimination, by 1980 the wages of black women equaled those of white women, and the adjusted differential between white and black men was less than half the difference between white men and white women. During the 1960s and 1970s, race differences in earnings decreased dramatically but sex differences did not.

Women earn much less than men at every level of education; the gap is as large for college graduates as for workers who have not finished high school. The differential does, however, vary systematically with age. When men and women first enter the work force, the gap in earnings is usually only about 10 or 15 percent. The gap widens rapidly as men and women move through their twenties and thirties, and then stabilizes after the age of 40. This age pattern has prevailed for at least the past half-century—but may be less true in the future. The current cohorts of young women are much more likely to remain in the work force during their twenties and thirties, continuing to invest in their careers. Thus, their earnings at this stage of the life cycle may show a growth pattern more similar to men's.

Table 3.4.   Ratios of hourly earnings, 1980.[a]

	Unadjusted (in percent)	Adjusted for differences in education (in percent)
Women as percent of men		
All	59	60
Whites	58	60
Blacks	75	71
Blacks as percent of whites		
Women	97	100
Men	76	85

a. Calculated from a 1 percent sample of the 1980 Census of Population. Throughout this book, estimates of hourly earnings or annual income are calculated from data covering the year prior to the year of the report—for example, the 1980 Census covers 1979 earnings.

We know that there are large sex differences in occupational patterns and that they contribute to the differences in earnings. However, the wage gap between women and men is very large even *within* more than 500 detailed Census occupations. The distributions in Table 3.5 show occupations grouped according to the wage ratios within each occupation, excluding those occupations which did not employ at least 2,500 workers in each of the comparison groups.

Most white men and women (74 percent) are employed in occupations in which the female-male wage ratio is between .50 and .69. Only 1 percent are in occupations with wage ratios of .90 or higher. By contrast, when black men are compared with white men, one-third are employed in occupations in which the earnings of black men are at least 90 percent of white men's, and another one-third are in the .80 to .89 range.

How is it possible for the wage gap between women and men to be so large *within* occupations when equal pay for equal work is the law of the land? The major reason is that the Census occupations usually include heterogeneous groups of workers who have different tasks. For example, the occupation "accountant" includes employees performing fairly routine auditing as well as highly skilled professionals with major responsibilities for advis-

Table 3.5.   Distribution of workers by wage ratios within occupations, 1980.

Wage ratio of white women to white men	Percent of white workers[a]	Wage ratio of black men to white men	Percent of men workers[a]
≥ 1.00	0.1	≥ 1.00	11
.90 to .99	1	.90 to .99	23
.80 to .89	9	.80 to .89	34
.70 to .79	14	.70 to .79	19
.60 to .69	43	.60 to .69	13
.50 to .59	31	.50 to .59	0.2
< .50	1	< .50	0.1

a. Percent distributions may not total exactly 100 because of rounding.

ing top management on a wide range of financial issues. A monograph on women and work concluded: "The workplace is substantially more segregated by sex than has been shown by studies of occupational concentration . . . A great degree of sex differentiation exists among the specific job titles included in the occupation" (Bianchi and Spain 1986, p. 165). Moreover, within an occupation the distribution of men and women by firm differs, and different firms frequently pay different wages for what is nominally the same occupation (Blau 1977).

Not only do women earn less than men on average, but an equally large differential emerges in direct husband-wife comparisons of individual couples. My analysis of white couples ages 25–64 (each spouse worked more than 1,000 hours in the previous year) revealed that three out of four husbands had hourly earnings greater than their wives, and for half the couples the wife's wage was less than two-thirds of her husband's (calculated from the March 1985 Current Population Survey). When both spouses are the same age and have the same education, the odds that the wife's hourly wage will be less than her husband's (3 to 1) exceed the probability that she will outlive him (about 2.3 to 1).

Discrimination

The facts about the wage gap are relatively uncontroversial, but there is great disagreement over why women earn so much less than men. Much of the controversy centers around the word "discrimination," a term that lends itself to a variety of conflicting interpretations. In the most general sense, discrimination means distinguishing among alternatives. The word often has a favorable connotation, as in "She is discriminating in her choice of friends." The unfavorable connotation is associated with distinctions that are made unfairly, or on the basis of irrelevant criteria. What is fair or relevant, however, is often a matter of subjective judgment. For instance, a life insurance company that charges cigarette smokers a higher premium than it charges nonsmokers is surely discriminating, but most people do not believe such a policy is unfair. Cigarette smoking is considered relevant because smokers have, on average, higher mortality rates than nonsmokers. On the other hand, life insurance companies are forbidden to charge men higher premiums than women (on the grounds that this would be discrimination), even though men on average do not live as long.

In economics there are at least two meanings of "discrimination": statistical discrimination and true wage discrimination. The former means evaluating individuals on the basis of group characteristics. It is not unfair for the group as a whole, but would understandably be seen as unfair by those members of the group whose true value is above the average. The latter means establishing wage differentials between groups of workers that cannot be explained by differences in the workers' contributions to employer revenues.

Does most of the earnings gap result from discrimination? In one sense the answer is surely yes. In another sense, no. So much depends on the meaning of the word "discrimination." What kind? By whom? When? Where? With what motive?

A hypothetical experiment may help clarify the issue. Suppose a large, random sample of baby girls were, from the moment of birth, perceived by everyone (including themselves) as boys. They would, on average, be shorter than other boys, and probably not as strong, but at home, in school, and in the workplace, they would be regarded as males. What would they earn as adults? Most likely their wages would be close to the average wages of men; it strains credulity to believe that they would be one-third less. But this means that the present large gap could be said to result from discrimination—that is, from the *response* that *gender* evokes—rather than from any inherent difference between women and men. This discrimination begins in the nursery and is carried forward in families, schools, churches, and every other social institution. When a woman says, "I earn less *because* I am a woman," the ascription of causality is well founded.

Once it is recognized that women earn less than men because

of their sex and that the lower earnings contribute to inequality in other aspects of life, the frustration and anger that many women feel is understandable. On the other hand, it is a huge leap from the conclusion that sex has a major effect on earnings to the inference that *employer discrimination* is the major source of the wage differential. Such a leap ignores discrimination from other sources such as employees and consumers, and, more important, ignores all the social and familial forces that depress women's earning power.

Let's do another hypothetical experiment. Suppose that women and men workers were equally valuable to employers. Given the present wage gap, firms that employ women instead of men would save approximately one-third of their labor costs. In many firms labor costs are about one-third of total costs, and profits are about 10 percent of revenues. Thus, this saving would result in a *doubling* of profits, as in the following example:

	Labor costs	Total costs	Revenue	Profit
If firms employ:				
men	30	90	100	10
women	20	80	100	20

Any employer interested in increasing profits (or avoiding losses) would have a tremendous incentive to hire women in place of men. Some employers might let their prejudice against women get in the way of their desire for profits, but unless all employers were equally prejudiced, those who were less bigoted would have a large competitive advantage over those who were more bigoted.

Within any particular industry some firms have a higher proportion of women workers, and these firms typically pay lower wages. These interfirm wage differentials are a significant reason men earn more than women within the same occupation. But if women were as valuable as men to employers, the firms that persist in hiring men should be driven out of business by their competitors who hire women. And industries that employ mostly women should earn greater profits and attract more capital than industries that employ men. The absence of any evidence of this kind makes it difficult to attribute much of the wage gap to employer discrimination.

It is possible to develop a theoretical case to show that an employer who faces very little competition for labor could benefit from setting wages for different workers on a basis different from their value to the firm. For example, hospital nurses in a town with only one hospital might be vulnerable to that type of exploitation. When employers have this power over workers, however, it would often be to their advantage to discriminate against *men* because they are more likely to be committed to the labor market regardless of the wage that is offered them. As a practical matter, however, this issue of employer control of labor markets does not have much force. In most markets there are numerous employers who must, within reasonable limits, pay the going wage in order to attract and hold their share of well-qualified employees.

Indeed, the whole question of employer behavior takes on a different cast once it is realized that a firm that discriminates against women is discriminating in favor of men. Why should employers want to pay men more than they have to? If employers have the power to control wages, why don't they drive down the wages of men? The answer is that they don't pay men more than they have to, any more than they do women. "Perfect competition" exists only in theory, but even in the real world most firms must pay attention to supply and demand in setting wages.

No doubt many women, perhaps most women, have experienced some discrimination by some employer at some point in their careers. Destructive as these acts may be for individual women, however, they do not explain the huge wage gap between women and men in the aggregate. Consider the fact that millions of workers, both men and women, do not have their wages determined by employers at all: their earnings depend upon self-employment income, commissions, tips, piece rates, and other forms of compensation closely tied to individual performance. The sex difference in hourly earnings of such workers is just as large as among regular wage and salary employees (Table 3.6). Indeed, among the self-employed, the gap in hourly earnings is slightly larger than among the employed, according to calculations based on the 1980 Census data.

In the past, women were less likely than men to be self-employed or to hold commission sales jobs, and sometimes this was the result of prejudice. However, in one well-known case (the Equal Employment Opportunity Commission versus Sears, Roebuck), a Federal District Court emphatically rejected the charge of discrimination even though the commission sales positions were disproportionately held by men. The court noted that after years of investigation "EEOC was unable to produce one Sears employee to testify that Sears discriminated against her by refusing to promote her to commission sales" (Commerce Clearing House, *Employment Practices Decisions,* p. 40-961).

Statistical Evidence

But aren't there numerous statistical studies that supposedly prove there is widespread employer discrimination? That depends on how the statistical results are interpreted. The typical study takes a sample of male and female workers and attempts to explain their individual earnings by their individual characteristics such as years of schooling, years of work experience, and so

Table 3.6. Women's hourly earnings as percent of men's, self-employed workers, 1980, ages 25–64.

	Unadjusted (in percent)	Adjusted for education (in percent)
All occupations[a]	53	57
Managerial	50	53
Professional	44	50
Sales	53	55
Service	56	56

a. Including groups not shown separately.

on. Most often, the characteristics used in the study explain only about half the difference in earnings between women and men. The unexplained portion is then attributed to employer discrimination.

Is this a reasonable inference? Probably not. One reason is that some of the characteristics controlled for in the studies may themselves be the result of discrimination. For instance, the analyst may control for whether the job requires supervision of other workers. But if employers discriminate against women in choosing supervisors, this type of analysis will underestimate the extent of discrimination.

On the other hand, simply labeling all of the unexplained portion of a statistical analysis "employer discrimination" is not very convincing. Consider an analogous attempt to explain sex differences in mortality. Suppose we took a sample of men and women who had died in a given year and attempted to explain variation in the age of death by individual characteristics such as cigarette smoking, education, income, and the like. Most of the seven-year gap in age of death between men and women would remain unexplained. Would we be justified in attributing the unexplained differential to discrimination against men by physicians and hospitals? Surely not. The statistical analysis shows that some individuals die sooner than others because they are men, but it does not tell us why. The explanation probably lies in some variables (for example, hormones or stress) that were not included in the analysis, but the exact reasons for the sex gap in mortality are not known.

Similarly, the statistical analysis of wages shows that some individuals earn less than others because they are women, but it doesn't tell us why. The difficult but central question is, "What is it about being a woman that leads to lower earnings?" The next chapter addresses that question.

Chapter 4

Trade-Offs and Tensions

In the 1960s and 1970s women were told that they could "have it all," but in the 1980s this concept has been painfully reappraised. Women are now warned against trying to be "super mom," and are urged to be more realistic concerning the trade-offs and tensions that they face. The change in perspective was described succinctly by Anna Quindlen, who gave up a major post at the *New York Times* to become a part-time columnist and married mother of two preschoolers: "Betty Friedan wrote in *The Feminine Mystique* that the question for women in those times was 'Is this all?' Now, of course, we feel differently. I *hope* this is all, because I can't handle any more" (1987, p. 17). And Sara Davidson expressed the frustrations of millions of women when she wrote, "All my time is spent on three things: baby, work, and keeping the marriage going. I find I can handle two beautifully . . . but three pushes me to the edge" (1984, p. 60).

Marriage and children severely handicap women's efforts to earn as much as men, and success in paid work usually requires great sacrifices by women. The conflict between family and career appears to be much greater for women than for men, and the persistence of that conflict continues to frustrate women's quest for economic equality.

"I Do" Has a Price

The tremendous impact of marriage and related homemaking responsibilities on women's wages is evident in a comparison of the hourly earnings of married and unmarried women at different ages. Figure 4.1 shows that in their early twenties married women actually earn slightly more than those who are unmarried, but their relative position deteriorates rapidly as they get older and their home responsibilities increase. By the time they are in their forties, the married women are making only 85 percent as much as the unmarried per hour of work.

Later in life, married women's relative position improves somewhat, probably because childcare responsibilities have di-

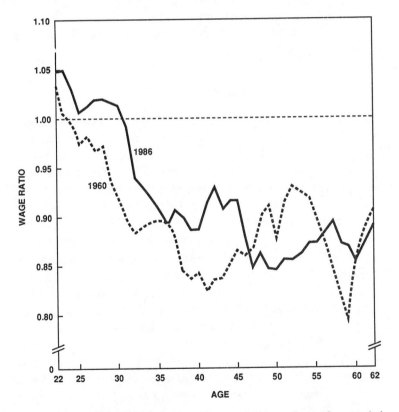

Figure 4.1 Wages of married white women relative to those of unmarried white women, by age (wages adjusted for education, and smoothed with five-year moving average).

minished and it is easier for them to devote their energies to paid jobs. Also, at that age the ranks of the unmarried are being increased by divorced (and widowed) women who, when they were married, faced the usual obstacles to careers. The life cycle pattern was similar in 1986 and 1960, except that the period of rapid decline in the ratio comes at a slightly later age in 1986. This shift may reflect a trend toward later childbearing.

In contrast to women, married men earn more than unmarried men at every age. The differential was much smaller in 1986 than in 1960 because in 1986 most of the unmarried (62 percent at ages 40–44) had been previously married, whereas in 1960 most (69 percent) were *never* married. The latter typically earn less than widowed or divorced men.

The Hidden Cost of Children

Having children entails numerous costs—expenditures for goods and services, time lost from paid work, and so on. In addition to these well-known, obvious costs, there is another that falls particularly on women in the form of *lower wages*. This happens for several reasons. First, many women leave the labor market during pregnancy, at childbirth, or when their children are young. These child-related interruptions are damaging to subsequent earnings because three out of four births occur to women before the age of 30—the same time that men are gaining the training and experience that lead to higher earnings later in life. Second, even when mothers stay in the labor force, responsibility for children frequently constrains their choice of job: they accept lower wages in exchange for shorter or more flexible hours, location near home, limited out-of-town travel, and the like. Third, women who devote a great deal of time and energy to childcare and associated housework are often less able to devote maximum effort to market work. For instance, when a young child is present, women are more likely than men to be absent from work, even at equal levels of education and wages (Leigh 1983, p. 360). According to Reskin and Hartmann, "The care of children . . . still appears to be largely women's responsibility, and this responsibility undoubtedly conflicts with their entrance into and advancement in a number of occupations that routinely require overtime, job-related travel, or inflexible or irregular hours" (1986, p. 134).

Perhaps most important of all, because most young women expect to be mothers, they (and their parents) are less likely than men to invest in wage-enhancing human capital while in school and in their first job or two after leaving school. In the past this has been reflected in choice of major, in uncertainty about pursuing graduate school training, and in a reluctance to experience the long hours and other rigors characteristic of apprenticeships in medicine, law, business, and other financially rewarding occupations. The difference between women and men in this respect is narrowing, partly because the barriers of prejudice are weakening, but also because more women are planning to remain childless and those who do want to become mothers expect to have fewer children and to spend less time with them. It is only the extraordinary woman who can succeed in a demanding career while doing full justice to the needs of spouse and children. Most men have never even tried.

The large impact of children on women's wages can be seen in Figure 4.2 which summarizes the relationship between hourly earnings and the number of children in the household. The analysis was restricted to white women in their thirties who worked at least 1,000 hours per year. Compared to childless women, those with children earn considerably less per hour, and wages drop appreciably with each additional child. Women with more children tend to have less education, but the adverse effect of children on wages is still strong when the analysis adjusts for years of schooling. (Control for potential sample selection bias concerning which women work at least 1,000 hours had no statistically significant effect on the results holding education constant.) The patterns in 1986 and 1960 are very similar; earnings fall significantly with each additional child. Similar analyses for men revealed no systematic relation between number of children and earnings.

Even women with no children earn substantially less than men.

When they were young, most of them did not know that they would be childless; their choice of subjects in school and their choice of job after leaving school probably did not differ much from those of other women. Similarly, prospective employers were unlikely to know which young women would have children and which would not. This uncertainty could affect the employer's willingness to provide training opportunities or to make other investments in job-related human capital. A British study of family responsibilities and pay differentials notes, "The expectation of a domestic division of labour between men and women encourages a sex-stereotyping in education and the labour market which puts all women, whether or not they ever become mothers, at a disadvantage relative to men" (Joshi and Newell 1987, p. 6).

Uncertainty about children does not end quickly for either

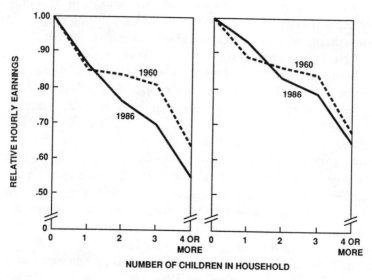

Figure 4.2 Relative hourly earnings of white women by number of children in household. Limited to women ages 30–39 who worked at least 1,000 paid hours (childless women = 1.00). Left: controlling for age. Right: controlling for age and education.

women or their employers. Consider women who are childless at age 30. According to current fertility patterns, one in four will have at least one child by the time she is 35. Thus, the observed association between women's hourly earnings and number of children underestimates the full effects of children. If baby girls came into the world with a stamp on their shoulder showing the number of children that they would ultimately bear, the relationship between women's earnings and their number of children would be much stronger than the one we observe in a world full of uncertainty. Childless women might still earn less than men, and some of that differential might be the result of employer discrimination, just as some might result from discrimination by consumers or other employees. The main point, however, is that at the ages when crucial decisions must be made about education and early job choices, most women do not know how many children they will have, to say nothing of the timing of those births.

The uncertainty about children is well illustrated by the 1986 survey of the Wellesley College class of 1966. More than half of the respondents from this all-women college said the number of children they have is different from the number they expected to have twenty years earlier. Three-fourths of those had fewer children than they originally expected; one-fourth had more. Moreover, one out of four survey respondents said that they currently hoped to have more children, indicating that uncertainty persists long after graduation from college.

The effect of children on women's earnings shows up in many studies, both in the United States and abroad. Economist Heather Joshi, in a study of British data (1986), has concluded that responsibility for childcare decreases women's earnings as much through loss of experience and training as through loss of pay during the time spent out of the work force. A Columbia University economist found that even the *timing* of births affects women's earnings. According to David Bloom (1987), women who delay childbearing beyond age 27 earn more than those who have children before 22, after controlling for education and work experience. But delay may have a price also, in terms of greater difficulty in conceiving and carrying successfully to term. "Physicians and the public should be taught that some degree of reproductive loss is normal and that the best insurance against being childless may be not to allot too short a period for childbearing" (Warburton 1987, p. 160).

Women's homemaking responsibilities reduce their earnings, and, in a feedback loop, the lower earnings induce behavior that further depresses women's labor market opportunities. For example, when couples move to a new city, the husband's career considerations usually dominate the decision (Frank 1978). After the move, the wife is less likely to resume work right away and frequently has difficulty finding an appropriate job. This bias reflects the economic reality that so long as men earn a great deal more than women, it is income-maximizing for the couple to place greater weight on the husband's career. A 10 percent wage gain for *him* is usually worth more to the couple than a 15 percent loss for *her*. If wives earned as much as husbands, however, this bias in location decisions would tend to disappear.

For many women the trade-off between career and family is only implicit, but an increasing number are keenly aware of the choices they must make and the consequences of those choices. One divorced mother, looking back on the numerous times she made career compromises in order to fulfill her obligations to her son, told me, "It was worth every dollar I didn't make."

What Price Progress?

Equal pay for equal work became the law of the land in the early 1960s, but the women/men wage gap persisted. If employer discrimination had been widespread prior to the passage of these laws, the gap should have narrowed, but between 1960 and 1980 the ratio remained remarkably stable. During the next six years, however, there was an unprecedented increase in the ratio of seven percentage points.

Why did women do so well after 1980? More vigorous enforcement of the antidiscrimination laws is not the answer. Betty

Friedan's critique of the Reagan administration—"There has been a consistent gutting of the machinery enforcing the laws on sex discrimination and employment" (1987, p. 1)—may be excessive, but there is no reason to think that enforcement increased. Moreover, women's relative gains were not particularly attributable to men's losses in industries such as steel or in regions such as the Midwest which were very depressed in the early 1980s. Between 1980 and 1986 the women/men wage ratio rose about seven percentage points in all industry groups, all occupational groups, and in all regions of the country. The gain was not, however, uniform at different ages, and this variation provides some clues regarding the reasons for the change.

In Figures 4.3 and 4.4 the women/men wage ratios, and the change in the ratio, are plotted for single years of age. The underlying series have been smoothed with a five-year moving average to reduce random variations, and have been adjusted for any sex difference in years of schooling. (The smoothed value for any year is obtained by taking an average of the value for that year, the two years preceding it, and the two years following it.) Between 1980 and 1986, women's relative earnings improved at all

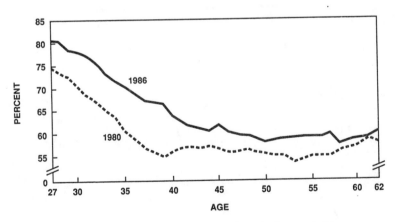

Figure 4.3 Women's wages as percentage of men's, by age (whites, wages adjusted for education, and smoothed with five-year moving average).

stages of the life cycle, but the gain was much greater for those under 40 years of age. The largest gains were recorded for the cohorts who were born in 1946–1950 and were in their late thirties in 1986. The women in these cohorts were the first to alter significantly their expectations and behavior with respect to work and family. They had substantially fewer children and were much more likely to divorce than the women who were born only half a decade earlier.

The higher an individual goes in business or the professions, the more intense is the conflict between career and family—for women, but not for men. Consider the results of two surveys of corporate officers by executive search firms (*Wall Street Journal* 1986, p. 1). The men were, on average, older than the women: 51 years versus 44. Both sexes worked about fifty-five hours per week on average. The men earned $215,000 per year; the women $117,000. Most significant, 20 percent of the women had never married, another 20 percent were divorced or separated, and more than half were childless. By contrast, over 99 percent of the men had married, 95 percent were fathers, and only 4 percent

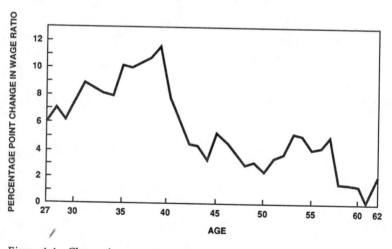

Figure 4.4 Change in women's wages as percentage of men's wages, by age (1986 minus 1980).

were separated or divorced. To be sure, not all women want to marry or want to have children, but four out of five of the women officers said they made personal sacrifices to advance their careers.

Even more modest success in paid work frequently requires women to trade off between family and career. Consider the 1.5 million white women in their thirties who earned over $25,000 in 1986. More than half of them were childless, compared with 24 percent of those making less than $25,000 and only 9 percent of those not in paid work. Many men in their thirties were also childless (28 percent of those making over $25,000 in 1986), but the trade-offs and tensions are not nearly as severe for men as for women. As we shall see, the absence of children seems to be felt more strongly by women, and the presence of children puts more pressure on them than on men.

The Demand for Children

According to some economists, women's greater commitment to childcare is a rational response of women and men based on *comparative advantage*. (This is an economic theory that explains specialization among countries, regions, or individuals by their relative efficiency in alternative activities; see Becker 1981, pp. 21–25.) This explanation is unsatisfactory. Even if comparative advantage could explain why women tend to specialize in performing one set of tasks and men another, it could not explain why this division of labor puts women at an economic disadvantage. Specialization and division of labor are present in most partnerships. In advertising agencies, for instance, one partner may be responsible for the artwork while another writes the copy; in dress manufacturing companies, one partner is usually in charge of production while another handles sales. In none of these cases, however, is there any presumption that one partner has more power than the other or that dissolution of the partnership will systematically place one partner at a disadvantage relative to the other.

Marriage is also a form of partnership with division of labor, but specialization alone cannot explain why one partner—the woman—is usually at a disadvantage. Suppose women were better than men at producing and caring for children but had no particular desire to do so, while it was men who wanted the children and cared more about their welfare. We would probably still see the same division of labor we see now, but men would have to pay dearly for women's services. The present hierarchy of power would be reversed.

The hypothesis most consistent with the facts is that, on average, women have a stronger demand for children than men do, and have more concern for their children after they are born. In short, there is a difference on the side of preferences, and this difference is a major source of women's economic disadvantage. Biological constraints on the timing of childbearing may contribute to this differential because would-be mothers in their late thirties feel that time is running out, whereas fatherhood remains a possibility for most men for much of their life.

The evidence concerning a gender difference with respect to children is not air-tight, but its appearance in so many different contexts makes this explanation more credible than any other that has been proposed. For instance, the large number of children born to, and living with, single mothers tells us something about women's desire for children. I estimate that about half of these births were *intended* at the time of conception. (Planned Parenthood surveys suggest that approximately four out of five conceptions among unmarried women are unintended. The statistics on legal abortions performed on unmarried women suggest that three out of four unintended conceptions are aborted. Thus, there would be approximately one unintended and one intended birth from the original five conceptions.) Moreover, even unmarried mothers who did not intend to become pregnant overwhelmingly prefer to raise their children themselves rather than give them up for adoption. The media frequently portray unwed motherhood as a teenage phenomenon, but two-thirds of these births are to women age 20 or older, and 30 percent are to women 25 or older.

Economic factors such as better labor market opportunities for women or government transfer programs make unwed motherhood more viable, but it would be foolish to ignore the psychological and even physiological satisfaction that women seek and often get from having babies. There is, writes journalist Anne Taylor Fleming, "a yearning for closeness that isn't always possible with a man, even a husband. That's what babies are giving women, as they no doubt gave them for centuries, a love with no lines, with an intimacy that is easier and often sweeter than sex" (1986, p. 34).

Residential custody patterns for children of divorced parents are also an indication of women's demand for children. A study of divorces in two California counties between September 1984 and March 1985 revealed that in three-quarters of the families there was joint *legal* custody, but in only 20 percent of the cases was *residential* custody joint between mother and father. In the other 80 percent of cases, the mother was fourteen times as likely as the father to have custody. The authors write, "To our surprise we are *not* seeing an increase in father custody" (Maccoby, Mnookin, and Depner 1986, p. 6).

What about men? Don't they also desire children and care about their welfare? Of course many do, some more so than the average woman. Each sex has its own distribution of preferences, and these distributions overlap. Although many men care a great deal, *on average* their desire and their caring do not seem to be as strong as women's. Hundreds of thousands of children born to unwed mothers never see their fathers or even know who they are. Many divorced fathers see their children rarely and contribute little or nothing to their support. Maternal abandonment of children is a relatively rare phenomenon, but paternal abandonment is not. When parents divorce and remarry, continuing contact between children and their mothers seems to be more important than contact with their biological fathers (Zill 1987). In their study of custodial arrangements following divorce, Maccoby and Mnookin find that the noncustodial mothers tend to maintain closer contact with their children than do noncustodial fathers (personal communication from Eleanor Maccoby, October 23, 1987).

Why is women's role in reproduction and parenting different from men's? Anyone interested in gender equality must be careful about invoking biological explanations (they have often been misused to justify inequality), but in this case it seems unlikely that the special concern of most mothers for their children is simply something that society thrusts upon them. Consider, for instance, the current controversy and concern over surrogate mothering. The sale of semen by men for the purpose of artificial insemination has been going on for decades without large-scale social debate. But the female part of reproduction—the sale of egg and womb—is correctly seen as much more significant and fraught with important personal and social consequences.

Socialization undoubtedly plays a role as well, but the experience of the Israeli kibbutzim shows how difficult it is to change traditional patterns of behavior. Most kibbutzim were founded with a strong commitment to gender equality in the assignment of jobs and to collective care of children, but traditional sex roles are very much in evidence. Childcare has always been predominantly in the hands of women, and direct ties between children and their parents have increased. Even the most ideologically committed group—the left-wing Artzi movement—voted in 1986 for "family accommodation." This means the children can leave their dormitories at night and sleep in their parents' rooms. According to a press report, "The pressure for change came mostly from young mothers, who also mobilized their husbands to vote in favor" (*Northern California Jewish Bulletin* 1987, p. 16).

The difference in parenting is probably related to the role difference in reproduction. Essayist Phyllis Theroux, for instance, describes giving birth and starting to nurse. She says that she pretended to visitors that she was the same and then adds, "But I was not the same, and I am still living out the differences. It is difficult to say what those differences are precisely, but they are bone deep" (1987, p. 15). Erica Jong, a long-time feminist, questions how strongly women really want men to take over parenting. She writes: "We long for men to share these tasks with us equally, but not only do they not *want* to, but we probably do not want to *relinquish* them. We are as attached to our children as ever. Liberation has not severed the umbilical cord—nor would we want it to" (1983, p. 3).

My conclusion that women's concern for children is, on average, greater than men's clarifies how child allowances or childcare subsidies help women, regardless of marital status. It is easy to see why a subsidy for childcare would improve the welfare of a single mother raising children alone. But what about a married mother whose family's taxes would increase by as much as the value of the subsidy? Why do most of these women also view such a policy as improving their situation even though there is clearly no gain for the family as a whole? The usual answer— "Because the woman is providing the care"—is incorrect, or at best seriously incomplete. The benefits of a childcare subsidy redound primarily to the person who *demands* the care, not to the one who *supplies* it.

Consider a couple who are *bargaining* (explicitly or implicitly) over how the household's income will be spent and how household chores will be allocated. *Game theory* assumes that, other things held constant, the strength of each participant in the bargaining situation will depend on how well off each would be if they fail to reach agreement—in this case, if they divorce. (Game theory is a theoretical approach to interactive decision making, used in economics to analyze situations where prices and quantities are the outcome of bargaining by individual participants, rather than the automatic result of a competitive market.) The stronger the individual's situation outside marriage, the stronger his or her bargaining position within marriage. If the woman is more concerned about the children than the man, a publicly supported childcare program will leave her better off in the event of divorce than if no such program existed. When her alternative as a divorced woman is better, her bargaining position—and her well-being—as a married woman is also improved.

Another way of seeing the logic of the argument is to consider the situation of a man who is left with small children through the death of his wife. Suppose that their care is of concern to him; he may remarry in order to obtain a stepmother to provide that care. (In the eighteenth and nineteenth centuries, when death rates for young and middle-aged women were much higher than now, widowers often remarried precisely for this reason.) Now imagine the effect on such a man and his new spouse (or potential spouse) if there is a new public childcare program supported by a flat tax per adult. If he has not yet remarried, he has less incentive to do so once the childcare program is in place. If he has remarried, he has less incentive to remain married. This example shows that it is the one who wants the childcare, not the one who provides it, who is the principal beneficiary of the public program.

In the early years of the sex-role revolution there was a hope that differences in homemaking and childcare responsibilities would disappear, but this is not occurring on a large scale. There are some households in which the father does as much as or more than the mother, but they are the exceptions, not the rule. Moreover, almost one child in four is raised in a household without father or stepfather. Children are still predominantly women's concern.

What about the future? My surveys of Stanford undergraduates reveal that they expect large sex-role differentials in homemaking and childcare to continue. These students live on a relatively nonsexist campus of an elite university. According to the responses to the surveys, careers are as important to the women as to the men; but when asked for their expectations about the allocation of time after marriage, the women say they expect to do about twice as much unpaid work as their husbands. This answer is completely consistent with the independent replies from the men; they expect to do half as much as their wives. The current ratio for all American women and men ages 25–64 in the aggregate is about 2.3 to 1.

Swedish experience also provides some clues about future developments in the United States, because many years ago Sweden enacted legislation (such as parental leave) that American women are still hoping for. The parental leave laws in Sweden cover fathers as well as mothers, but in only one couple in five does the man take the leave. Furthermore, a 1983 survey of household time use showed Swedish women spending five times as much time on childcare as Sweden's men (*Sweden Now* 1986). The ratio in the United States for childcare is about 3.5 to 1. (See Chapter 5, below.)

Tension within the Home

In 1960 most women and men ages 25–44 lived in so-called traditional households: they were married, there was at least one child, and the husband had a paid job while the wife did not. In these households the wife usually did almost all of the housework and childcare; the husband worked an equivalent number of hours in the labor market. Husbands and wives usually consumed approximately equal amounts of goods and services, but the marriage was often unequal in many other respects. The husband typically had more control over important decisions and enjoyed a degree of freedom not available to the wife. In earlier eras the husband's control over his wife was not only based on economics but was sanctioned by religion and enforced by law. In modern times, his control is derived primarily from his greater earning power and her need for a provider for her children. A large-scale study of American couples noted that "in traditional marriages, interdependence is usually achieved at the cost of the wife's autonomy and her participation on an equal basis in decision making" (Blumstein and Schwartz 1983, p. 109).

By 1986 the "traditional" family was distinctly in the minority. Current Population Survey data show that at ages 25–44 only one woman in four was a married mother without a paid job. The proportion not married had jumped from one in six to almost one in three. Equally important was the surge of married mothers into paid jobs. Their increase in hours of paid work, however, was not accompanied by an equivalent assumption of responsibility for housework and childcare by men. Disputes over who does what have become an increasing source of tension, fulfilling Rebecca West's prediction that "the great enemy of feminism is that men don't like housework and women don't like housework" (Ms. 1987, p. 142). According to psychologist Morton H. Shaevitz, an expert on gender relations, "Arguments about housework are the leading cause of domestic violence in the United States" (*Healthcare Forum* 1987, p. 27).

Sex-role differences in *responsibility* are often as big a burden for women as differences in actual hours of work. When both parents have paid jobs, it is usually the mother who gets called when a child gets sick at school, the mother who must reschedule when the babysitter fails to show, and the mother who is, in fact, the "family manager." How can women compete with men in the labor market when "for many women it is proving extremely difficult to decide whether they are mainly mothers who happen to work, or workers who happen to be mothers?" (O'Connell and Bloom 1986, p. 9.)

In summary, most women face a serious dilemma. If they devote themselves to housework and childcare, they are likely to have to assume a subordinate role in a hierarchical marriage. Moreover, full-time homemakers run the risk that divorce will leave them with inadequate skills for earning a living at a paid job. On the other hand, if women seek to compete with men in the labor market, the experience to date suggests that most will have to make substantial sacrifices with respect to marriage and children. The next chapter constructs a balance sheet to determine whether the changes in market work and family of recent decades have brought women any closer to economic equality.

Chapter 5

The Balance Sheets of Economic Well-Being

The fifteenth anniversary issue of *Ms.* (July/August 1987) celebrated the progress that American women have made in the past few decades and credited much of that progress to the women's movement. Gloria Steinem, a founder and editor of *Ms.*, wrote of a "quantum leap forward from fifteen years ago, when independence for women was ridiculed as the unnatural idea of a few 'bra burners'" (p. 55). She mentions specifically the transformation of the paid labor force in the 1970s and 1980s and the increasing representation of women in elective offices.

Other observers have been less sanguine about the effects on women of recent changes in gender roles and relationships. They point to the rise in the number of women who are divorced or never married and the increase in childlessness, although not all women consider these to be disadvantages. The failure of many divorced men to pay alimony or child support is clearly a negative phenomenon, as is the hostility of some men toward women as expressed in rape and physical abuse. There has been frequent mention of the "feminization" of poverty (Bane 1986) with the implication that at least some women have been hurt economically. According to the heroine of Nora Ephron's novel *Heartburn,* "the major concrete achievement of the women's movement in the 1970s was the Dutch treat" (1983, p. 81).

Are women better off now than they were in 1960? Are they worse off? A complete answer to this question—one that takes account of feelings of self-worth, autonomy, and other psychological dimensions—is beyond the scope of this book and is probably impossible. The sources of well-being are so numerous—love, work, health, family, friendships, religion—and their interactions so complex as to defy measurement and aggregation. Many women have testified eloquently to their enhanced feelings of self-worth, to their ability to function independently, to an enlarged sense of power and autonomy. At bottom, however, no one can ever quantify another person's misery or joy.

It is possible, however, to address a more restricted set of questions concerning *economic well-being,* which economists usually define as access to goods, services, and leisure. Here I will build on my previous discussions of employment, wages, and family in order to answer the question "Did women improve their economic position relative to men between 1960 and 1986?" Despite large structural changes in the economy and major antidiscrimination legislation, the economic well-being of women as a whole (in comparison with men) did not improve. The women/men ratio of *money income* almost doubled, but women had less leisure while men had more, an increase in the proportion of adults not married made more women dependent on their own income, and women's share of financial responsibility for children rose. One group of women, however, did achieve great gains relative to their male counterparts. They were unmarried, white, young, and well educated.

The second part of the chapter tackles the question of the feminization of poverty. The claim that there has been a large increase in the percent of adult poor who are women is true for blacks but not for whites. The claim that feminization has accelerated in recent years (Pearce and McAdoo 1984) is not supported for either race. There was considerable feminization of poverty in the 1960s, but in the 1970s the sex mix of poverty was relatively constant for whites, and between 1980 and 1986 women's share decreased. Among blacks, feminization of poverty continued in the 1970s, and then held constant in the 1980s. An increase in the proportion of women in households without men was the principal source of feminization of poverty for both races, and the principal reason the trend was more adverse for blacks than for whites.

Economic Well-Being

What determines a person's economic well-being? It obviously depends on money income, because money is needed to buy goods and services that are produced in the market. It also depends on access to goods and services produced outside the market; no one should imagine that when a man or woman substitutes a paid job for housework and childcare that the household's economic well-being increases by the full value of the money income. In addition, economists include leisure in the definition of economic well-being: a person who works 70 hours per week at $10 per hour is not twice as well off as one who works 35 hours per week at the same wage. Finally, economic well-being depends on the size and structure of the household and the extent of income sharing within that household.

The comparisons that follow focus on men and women between the ages of 25 and 64—when gender-role differences tend to be greatest. Adults at these ages are most likely to be in the labor market and most likely to be responsible for children. Details concerning the methods of estimation are provided in an appendix to this chapter.

Hours of Work

The paid work hours of women compared with men rose substantially between 1960 and 1986, primarily because the proportion of women with paid jobs jumped from 34 to 57 percent (see Table 5.1). A second factor was the decline in the proportion of men working at paid jobs: from 87 to 80 percent. Third, and least important, there was a slight increase in the average annual hours of those women who were employed (from 1,677 to 1,750), while hours per employed man were unchanged at 2,153 per year.

Housework hours fell for women while remaining virtually constant for men; childcare hours fell for both sexes. The fall in childcare hours for men may surprise some readers who know of individual families in which the father now provides as much or more care than the mother. There are probably more such families in the 1980s than there were in 1960, but two other trends work in the opposite direction. First, the proportion of men who have *no* children jumped substantially (from 27 to 47 percent at ages 25–39) between 1960 and 1986. Second, among those who do have children, the number of children per man fell from 2.4 to 1.8. Thus, hours of paternal care per child would have had to almost double in order for the *average childcare per man* in 1986 to equal that of 1960. For every married man who currently does as much housework and childcare as his wife, there is at least one divorced or never-married father who seldom sees his children, and another who has opted to have no children at all.

When the various types of work are summed, we find that women increased their total hours by almost 7 percent, while men's fell by that same proportion. As a result, by 1986 women were putting in more hours of work than men, whereas in 1960 the reverse was true. The differential change was particularly large for married couples: on average, wives increased their total work load by four hours per week while husbands decreased theirs by two and a half hours. Unmarried women work more hours (total of paid and unpaid) than unmarried men, but the differential did not change much between 1960 and 1986.

Table 5.1.   Average annual hours of work.

	Year	Paid	Housework	Childcare	Total
Women	1960	572	1,423	266	2,261
	1986	997	1,222	197	2,416
Men	1960	1,875	542	76	2,493
	1986	1,725	545	58	2,328
Women/men ratio	1960	.30	2.62	3.52	.91
	1986	.58	2.24	3.40	1.04

Income

The average money income received by women rose by 140 percent between 1960 and 1986, while men showed a gain of only 25 percent (see Table 5.2). These are real increases because all dollar figures for 1960 have been inflated to 1985 dollars by the Consumer Price Index. The women/men ratio of money income almost doubled, primarily because of the large differential change in hours of paid work and secondarily because of an increase of about seven percentage points in the women/men wage ratio.

The women/men ratio of imputed income from housework declined, following the trend in the housework hours ratio. No income was imputed for childcare hours because they do not result in goods or services for the adult men and women whose economic well-being is being estimated. To be sure, childcare may be a source of pleasure to the adult who provides it, but that can be true of paid work as well.

Women's total income rose faster than men's, but the ratio was still only .66 in 1986, a year when the average woman worked more hours (paid plus unpaid) than did the average man.

Effective Income

Almost 90 percent of women and men ages 25–64 live in households with other adults or children, or both; this affects their access to goods and services in several ways. First, larger households can usually realize *economies of scale* (make more effective use of income) through joint use of housing, durable goods, and services. Thus, the effective income resulting from any given amount of money and imputed income tends to rise with household size. Second, if there are children present, some income must be devoted to them, thus reducing the effective income available to the adult members of the household. Third, the adults in the household may, to a greater or lesser extent, share their income, thus increasing or decreasing the effective income of individuals relative to their own income.

Assuming that income is equally shared, women have almost

as much as men but their relative position declined by two percentage points between 1960 and 1986 (see Table 5.3). This decline is primarily the result of the increase in the percentage of women who are not married and therefore not benefiting from the higher income of a husband.

The average levels and changes in the averages are an accurate reflection of the entire distribution of women relative to the average (median) man, as can be seen in Figure 5.1. The central tendency is slightly below 1.0 in both years, and the distribution shifted slightly to the left (the women/men ratio fell) between 1960 and 1986, except for a small increase in the proportion of women with ratios over 2.0 from 7.3 to 7.8 percent. The latter change reflected a general increase in inequality; the proportion

Table 5.2.   Average annual income (1985 dollars).

	Year	Money	Imputed (housework)	Total
Year	1960	4,469	9,275	13,744
	1986	10,738	10,611	21,413
Men	1960	10,273	5,547	25,820
	1986	25,378	7,019	32,396
Women/men ratio	1960	.22	1.67	.53
	1986	.42	1.51	.66

Table 5.3.   Effective income per person and per hour of work (1985 dollars, equal sharing).

Year	Women	Men	Women/men ratio
Per person			
1960	23,868	24,452	0.98
1986	33,485	34,927	0.96
Per hour of work			
1960	10.56	9.81	1.08
1986	13.86	15.00	0.92

of men with more than two times the median man's income rose even more—from 7.5 to 8.7 percent.

Effective Income per Hour of Work

The final step in assessing economic well-being is to combine effective income (which measures access to goods and services) with leisure (time left after market and nonmarket work). One such measure that is simple to calculate and understand is effective income per hour of work (paid and unpaid). There are several other possible measures; they all yield the same qualitative

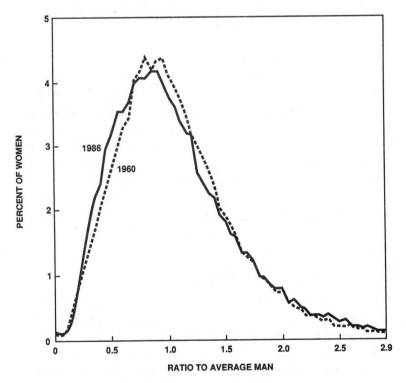

Figure 5.1 Frequency distribution for women, effective income relative to that of average man (equal sharing).

conclusions. For instance, one could sum effective income and the imputed value of leisure (set equal to the imputed wage of an hour of housework). The changes in the sex ratios of this measure are similar in direction and magnitude to the changes shown below.

In absolute terms women's effective income per hour of work rose between 1960 and 1986, reflecting the general rise in economic productivity (see Table 5.3). Relative to men, however, women's position fell substantially, from 1.08 to 0.92, primarily because of the increased burden of work on women who took paid jobs but still had substantial responsibilities at home. The data emphatically refute the view that women as a group have made great progress in their quest for economic equality.

Winners and Losers

The failure of women *on average* to advance does not mean that each and every subgroup had the same experience. Indeed, there is one special category of women that achieved a large increase in economic well-being relative to their male counterparts. They are white, young (ages 25–44), not married, and well educated (more than twelve years of schooling). If these women perceive considerable progress toward economic equality, they are correct. If, however, they believe that women as a whole have experienced this progress, they are in error. All other subgroups of women showed losses or very small gains (see Table 5.4).

Qualifications and Conclusions

The calculation of unpaid hours of work assumed that these hours depend upon such characteristics as age, sex, marital status, and age and number of children, and that the basic structure did not change for any given set of characteristics. Some observers have suggested that men have increased their hours of housework and childcare and point to stories about househusbands or families where unpaid work is shared equally. I believe these cases are atypical, but even if men's hours of housework and childcare in 1986 were 25 percent higher than my estimates, the women/men ratio of effective income per hour of work would still have declined between 1960 and 1986, from 1.08 to 0.98.

Another qualification concerns the assumption of equal sharing. Casual observation suggests that within a marriage spouses usually consume similar amounts of housing, food, clothing, and other goods and services, even when their contributions to total (money plus imputed) income are unequal. Another view, however, asserts that there is bargaining within households and that the bargaining power of each spouse depends, at least in part, on her or his contribution to the household's total income. Sociologist Kristin A. Moore and economist Isabel V. Sawhill discuss bargaining within marriage and suggest that women's greater earning power increases their ability to affect household choices—for example, "The wife who once had to ask her husband's permission to buy a new dress will be free to make her own decisions about these matters" (1976, p. 108). The key point is not that the family will necessarily spend more on

Table 5.4. Women/men ratio of effective income per hour of work (equal sharing).

	1960	1986
Blacks	0.96	0.78
Whites	1.09	0.94
Whites		
Married	1.16	1.03
Not married	0.74	0.73
25–34	1.02	0.91
35–44	1.14	0.98
45–54	1.16	0.98
55–64	1.03	0.91
25–44, not married, more than 12 years of schooling	0.72	0.81

dresses, but that the hierarchical character of the decision-making process is altered.

An extreme view is that control over goods and services varies in direct proportion to the contribution each individual makes to the household's total income: there is no sharing between adults; the only redistribution in the household is from adults to children. If we assume such "proportionate sharing," women's *level* of economic well-being is much worse than under equal sharing, because it depends primarily on their own income. The trend in the women/men ratio of effective income per hour of work, however, shows a small increase (from .59 to .62) between 1960 and 1986, primarily as a result of the narrowing of the wage gap in the 1980s.

Equal sharing and proportionate sharing can be viewed as polar cases. If one assumes that the truth lies somewhere in between, the conclusion of no gain for women still stands. For instance, an average of the two assumptions shows the women/men ratio falling from .84 to .77 between 1960 and 1986, or to .80 if the estimate of men's nonmarket hours in 1986 is increased by 25 percent.

In conclusion, with the exceptions and qualifications noted, the revolutionary changes of the past quarter-century did not bring women any closer to economic equality with men. It needs to be again emphasized, however, that the assessment of *economic* well-being does not capture all of the effects of the sex-role revolution. There may well have been gains in noneconomic dimensions; the data on work and income remind us that these gains have been achieved at a cost, and that the cost has varied greatly from one woman to another. Let us now look at the effects for women and men at the low end of the income distribution.

The Feminization of Poverty

We have seen that women did not improve their economic well-being relative to men between 1960 and 1986. What about the reverse? Did the situation worsen—at least for those women at the lower end of the income distributions? In particular, was there an increase in the proportion of the adult poor who are women, and if so, when did it occur and why? We will again focus on adults who are ages 25–64, the ages most useful for understanding gender differences in poverty. As explained in the appendix, measurement of poverty trends among very young and old adults are confounded by changes in living arrangements, the importance of noncash benefits, and other factors.

Results

Both sexes experienced a dramatic decline in the incidence of poverty in the 1960s and some additional decline in the 1970s. Between 1980 and 1986, however, the trend reversed, and poverty tended to increase. Blacks were three times as likely as whites to be poor, regardless of sex.

The percent of poor who were women increased substantially during the 1960s for all races and especially for blacks (see Table 5.5). After 1970 there was no further feminization of poverty for whites; in fact, in the 1970s and 1980s the percent of the poor who were women declined by as much as it had increased in the

Table 5.5. Poverty trends, ages 25–64.

	Census			Current Population Survey	
	1960	1970	1980	1980	1986
Percent living in poverty					
White women	14.8	8.7	7.7	8.3	9.7
White men	11.9	5.9	5.5	5.5	7.2
Black women	45.3	30.9	24.8	26.5	27.0
Black men	36.8	19.9	14.3	14.0	13.8
Women as percent of poor					
Whites	57.3	61.7	60.2	62.2	59.1
Blacks	59.2	66.1	69.3	72.4	72.4

1960s. Feminization of poverty continued for blacks until 1980 and held constant after that date.

Sources of Change

Why is the percentage of adult poor who are women always over 50 percent, and why does the percentage change over time? The answer to both questions is to be found in the distribution of men and women by type of household and the incidence of poverty in those households. On average, men earn appreciably more money than women, but if all men and women lived in two-sex households, the proportion of poor who are women would always be approximately one-half. It is the presence of one-sex households and the lower income of women with respect to men in those types of households that determine the feminization of poverty.

At ages 25–64 approximately one in five white women and four in ten black women in 1986 lived in households without men (see Table 5.6). The incidence of poverty in such households is appreciably higher than in households that have only men, or in households that include adults of both sexes. Poverty rates are especially high for women in households that have children but no men.

Table 5.6.   Women living in poverty, ages 25–64.

	Percent living in poverty		Percent of all women of that race	
	1960	1986	1960	1986
White women				
With children, no man	51	38	3	7
No children, no man	27	13	9	12
Black women				
With children, no man	78	58	15	24
No children, no man	57	26	10	15

The percent of the poor who are women depends on the poverty rate of each sex in each type of household multiplied by the proportion of the population in each type of household. Between 1960 and 1986 there was some increase in the percent of white women living without a man, but this was offset by substantial declines in the poverty rates for such households so that overall there was no feminization. Poverty rates also declined in black women's households, but the increase in the percent of black women living without men, and especially those with children, was so great as to result in considerable feminization.

Alternative Measures

How would these conclusions about the feminization of poverty be affected if alternative definitions of income and alternative assumptions about sharing were used? A shift from pretax to after-tax income would probably have little consequence because neither women nor men living in poverty pay much income tax. Similarly, failure to include an imputation for fringe benefits is probably not important because these benefits are likely to be small for the poor, and are usually approximately equal for men and women as a percent of labor income (Atrostic 1983). Noncash transfers such as food stamps and housing subsidies are relatively more important for women than for men; thus, their inclusion would tend to lower the percent of the poor who are women. However, most of these transfers go to people younger than 25 or older than 64.

Probably the most serious shortcoming of cash income as a measure of economic well-being is that it neglects the value of goods and services produced in the home. For all households (poor and nonpoor), the value of home production is about one-half of money income, with the proportion probably higher in low-income households and probably highest of all in female-headed households. Thus, inclusion of home production in the definition of income would tend to lower the percent of the poor who are women.

Taking the four possible modifications of the income measure together—taxes, fringe benefits, noncash transfers, and home production—it seems that the *level* of the percent of poor who are women would probably be lower than the figures presented in this chapter. The net trend in this statistic, however, would probably not be much affected because noncash transfers have tended to rise while home production has tended to fall.

Finally, there is the question of the sharing rule within households. If, instead of equal sharing, there were proportionate sharing, the percent of poor who are women would be much higher. There would, however, be a downward trend in the percentage over time because women's money income has been rising much more rapidly than men's. Between 1960 and 1980 it rose, primarily because women's employment rate was increasing while men's was decreasing. Between 1980 and 1986 the divergent employment trends continued and were reinforced by a substantial increase in the women/men ratio of hourly earnings.

Given these findings, why do so many believe that poverty has been feminized? One possibility is that the worsening economic position of children (relative to adults) is confounded with the position of women. The next chapter shows that the incidence of poverty among children has risen sharply, relative to the incidence among women or men. This is not primarily a result of the growth of female-headed families but reflects a relative fall in income of all households with children (Fuchs 1986c). If, as I have argued, women are more concerned about children than are men, it is important to note this disparity in assessing women's overall welfare. But in analyzing the problems of gender inequality and poverty, and in developing policies to deal with these problems, it is also useful to distinguish between poverty among women and among children.

In summary, both the analysis of poverty and the estimates of average economic well-being indicate that the relative position of women and men changed little between 1960 and 1986. Some women have gained—most notably those who are young, white, well educated, and unmarried. The biggest economic losses were suffered by black women, who are increasingly raising children without male financial support. Their position deteriorated despite the fact that their wages rose more rapidly than black men's or those of whites of either sex. The experience of black women should serve as an indication of the complex interrelations between the labor market and the family, and of the need to consider all aspects in trying to develop policies that would help women.

Appendix: Definitions, Sources, and Methods

Economic Well-Being

Estimates are made for 1960 from the Census of Population and for 1986 from the March Current Population Survey (CPS). Because the samples and methods used in the CPS differ slightly from those in the Census, the rates of change in the CPS from 1980 to 1986 were used to extrapolate the 1980 Census results to 1986, thus obtaining greater consistency with the 1960 Census.

Hours of Work

Annual hours of paid work for each employed individual are estimated directly from the Census and CPS reports. The number is the product of weeks worked in the previous year and hours worked in the survey week. This method may introduce error for individuals because of differences between hours in the same week and average weekly hours in the previous year, but the estimate for aggregates is relatively unbiased. Total hours for a group—for example, women—are divided by the number of people in the group, regardless of whether they had a paid job or not, in order to obtain average annual hours.

The unpaid (nonmarket) hours of work are much more difficult to estimate. We would like to know how much time each individual in the samples spent in housework (including cooking, cleaning, laundering, yard work, repairs, and maintenance) and in childcare, but neither the Census nor the CPS provides such information. Indeed, there is no source in or out of government that provides systematic measures of unpaid hours of work in 1960 and 1986. We must rely on an estimating procedure that is far from ideal but is vastly preferable to ignoring changes in unpaid work.

The best information on unpaid work comes from a survey conducted by the University of Michigan's Institute for Social Research in 1975–76. The Institute made available to me data from the time-use diaries kept by 776 individuals on four different days chosen to reflect weekday and weekend activity. I used regression analysis to determine how hours of housework and hours of childcare varied according to the sex of the individual, marital status, age, race, hours of paid work, and number and age of children.

The results were then applied to the characteristics of the individuals in the Census and CPS samples in 1960 and 1986. For example, a white married woman between 25 and 44 years of age who had no paid job and had two or more children with at least one under age 5 was estimated as having 1,756 hours of housework and 676 hours of childcare per year. A white woman of the same age who was not married, without children, and working 2,000 hours a year in a paid job, was estimated to have 621 hours of housework and no childcare hours. With this method of estimation, average hours of unpaid work change over time as the characteristics of the population change, but there is no change for any fixed set of characteristics. The possibility that men increased their nonmarket hours of work, holding characteristics constant, is considered by presenting alternative estimates that raise men's nonmarket hours by 25 percent.

Income

Annual money income of each individual reported in Census and CPS samples includes pretax cash income from all sources, including labor and nonlabor income as well as alimony, welfare payments, and other cash transfers. But just as paid hours of work does not measure the total workload of men and women, money income does not capture the total value of goods and services available to them and their families. Unpaid work such as housework also creates goods and services that enhance economic well-being; the problem is how to value it.

I follow the general approach found in most economic analyses of using wages in paid work to impute wages for unpaid work. Specifically, if an individual had at least 500 paid hours during the year, his or her market wage was used to value each hour of housework. For other individuals, an hour of housework was valued by the average hourly wage earned in paid jobs by workers of the same sex, race, age, and education. Two alternative calculations, valuing the housework hours of "nonworkers" at either 1.25 or 0.75 of the wages of their peers who had paid jobs, did not significantly affect the trends in women/men differentials in income.

Effective Income

To capture the effects of economies of scale and the presence of children, the number of "adult equivalents" for each household was assumed to vary in proportion to the official poverty threshold for each type of household. The Census Bureau sets the poverty threshold for each household based on the number of adults and number of children present. For instance, the poverty threshold for a household with two adults and two children in 1985 was $10,903, while the poverty threshold for a one-adult household with no children was $5,593. The ratio indicates 1.95 adult equivalents for the two-adult, two-child household. Several alternative methods of estimating adult equivalents were tried; all plausible schemes for weighting adults and children and taking account of economies of scale give similar results.

The results are sensitive, however, to assumptions about how income is shared within the household. I follow the standard assumption implicit in most economic analyses that the household members pool their income and share it equally. Under equal sharing, the effective income of each adult is given by the household's total income divided by the number of adult equivalents. Thus, each additional child reduces the effective income per adult because it increases the number of adult equivalents. An alternative assumption of proportionate sharing is also considered. Under this assumption, the effective income of each adult is equal to his or her *own* total income multiplied by the ratio of the number of adults to the number of adult equivalents in the household. This ratio simultaneously reflects the gain in effective income resulting from economies of scale and the loss in effective income to adults attributable to the presence of children.

Feminization of Poverty

Feminization of poverty is defined as an increase in the percentage of the adult poor who are women. An alternative definition—an increase in the probability of a woman's being poor relative to the probability of a man's being poor—yields very similar results. (The ratio of the probabilities of poverty is an arithmetical transformation of women's share of poverty if there are equal numbers of men and women.)

Income is defined as the pretax cash income from all sources received by members of a household in the previous year. Following the standard approach to the measurement of poverty, no imputation is made for nonmarket production (such as housework or childcare), fringe benefits (such as employer-paid health insurance premiums), or noncash transfers (such as food stamps). The possible effects of these factors on the feminization of poverty are discussed in the chapter.

The poverty levels for each household in each year are set according to the official Census Bureau weights that establish poverty thresholds based on the number of adults and number of children in the household. Once a household is identified as having total money income below the poverty threshold, all the individuals in that household are deemed to be living in poverty (according to the equal-sharing assumption).

The poverty trends are calculated for ages 25–64. Income comparisons at ages under 25 are not reliable guides to lifetime levels of economic well-being because many young adults are still in school; their current income may be much lower than their average lifetime income or their current level of living. Also, some young people choose their first full-time job partly for the experience and training it affords; therefore their nominal wage does not adequately measure their total compensation. If, for instance, there is a change in the women/men ratio of enrollment in colleges and graduate schools, money income measures at ages 18–24 may give a misleading picture of the true sex differences in economic circumstances. Money income can also be a biased measure of living standards at older ages, partly because the value of assets such as owner-occupied homes is not included. Also, noncash benefits such as subsidized housing and medical care are very significant for many of the low-income elderly. Perhaps most important, as Social Security and private pensions have improved the income position of the elderly, there has been a major movement of widows 65 and older to independent living (70 percent in 1985 compared with 40 percent in 1960). This massive change in living arrangements greatly complicates the interpretation of economic well-being.

Chapter 6

No One Is an Island

Conflicts between career and family bear heavily on many women, and their gains in paid work have been offset by loss of leisure and the decline of marriage. Young, white, well-educated, unmarried women have made substantial economic progress relative to their male counterparts, but the price has often included forgoing the opportunity to have a child. For the first time in our nation's history, an entire generation of young people are not replacing themselves. Furthermore, those women who do combine motherhood with paid work face constant pressures to arrange appropriate care for their children and frequent crises when those arrangements go awry.

Opinions differ as to whether women have, in some overall sense, improved their position relative to men during the past quarter-century. There is, however, little disagreement that recent decades have been particularly difficult ones for children. While many American children are flourishing in the new world of the 1980s, an increasing proportion are not. Compared with their parents' generation, children today commit suicide at a higher rate, perform worse in school, are more likely to be obese, and show other evidence of increased physical, mental, and emotional distress. The poverty rate among children is almost double the rate for adults—a situation without precedent in American history.

These trends are obviously of great importance to those directly involved, but their significance does not end there. The decisions that individual women and men make about marriage, parenthood, and the care of children have major implications for all Americans, including the tens of millions who do not directly participate in these decisions. This arena of behavior provides an example of the *externalities,* or "third-party effects," that economists have analyzed in other contexts.

An externality exists when the actions taken by a household or firm impose costs or confer benefits on other households or firms but there is no feasible way of arranging direct compensation for these costs or benefits. When externalities are present, the decisions made by the household or firm based on its *own* welfare will not be optimal from a *social* point of view. The household or firm presumably looks at its costs and benefits; the social optimum requires also taking into account the costs and benefits imposed on others.

A classic example of a negative externality is the cost of air pollution imposed on others by the smoke emanating from a factory. Unless restrained in some way, plant owners will tend to choose the cheapest fuel regardless of the costs imposed on others by pollution. An example of a positive externality is the effect on society of an individual's decision about vaccination for a communicable disease. The individual tends to look at the costs and benefits to her (or her child), and may ignore the benefit to others that flows from reduction in risk of the spread of the disease.

One way to deal with externalities is for the government to prohibit or require certain actions. For instance, the government may make vaccination mandatory. Another way is to modify the prices facing households or firms (through taxes or subsidies) so that the price properly reflects the social costs or benefits. For instance, the government allows homeowners to deduct real estate taxes and interest payments from taxable income in an effort to encourage home ownership, which is believed to have benefits for society as a whole. In principle, use of the price mechanism permits a much closer approximation to a social optimum than do universal requirements or proscriptions, but practical difficulties may preclude the price approach in some situations.

This chapter looks at the externalities involved in women's quest for economic equality with special emphasis on fertility and childcare. We will see that this is not just a "feminist" issue, but one that affects everyone. It is a situation well captured by John Donne's famous phrase: "No man is an Island, intire of itselfe; every man is a peece of the continent, a part of the maine."

Fertility

The Policy Issue

Americans are not reproducing themselves. Even during the early 1980s, when total births increased because the baby boomers were at the peak childbearing ages, the number of births per 1,000 women ages 15–44 still remained below replacement level. The facts are beyond dispute, but their implications for policy are not. One response is, "So what? If American women and men of childbearing age decide that they want small families or none at all, it's their business and no one else's." An alternative view is that the birthrate is of national concern, that the choices made by individuals are not necessarily in the best interests of society as a whole. Paul Demeny, in his presidential address to the Population Association of America in April 1986, said, "The essence of the population problem, if there is a problem, is that individual decisions with respect to demographic acts do not add up to a recognized common good—that choices at the individual level are not congruent with the collective interest" (1986, p. 473).

Demeny's statement is completely open-ended as to the direction of the possible discrepancy between individual and collective interests. In some countries the birth rate may be greater than is socially desirable; in other countries the rate may be just right, and in still others it may be too low. Which situation obtains depends on the distribution of costs and benefits of children between the private and collective interests (see Figure 6.1).

In a society in which fertility decisions are the result of deliberate choice, potential parents would normally compare private costs and benefits—that is, the values in boxes A and B in Figure 6.1. The social good requires that they also take into account the values in boxes C and D. If the collective costs exceed the collective benefits, children are creating a negative externality; if the reverse is true, the externality is positive. To achieve a fertility rate that would be best from a social point of view, a democratic government should use taxes (if the externality is negative) or subsidies (if the externality is positive) so that potential parents will, in effect, take the externalities into account in making their private decisions.

Whether children are a source of negative or positive externalities in the United States at present is under debate. Collective costs include public education, publicly provided health care, and the provision of other public services (such as police protection) whose costs tend to vary with population size. Many people are also concerned about the pressure of population on the environment and natural amenities.

The collective benefits of children can take several different

	COSTS OF CHILDREN	BENEFITS OF CHILDREN
PRIVATE INTEREST (parents)	**A** EXAMPLE: FOOD	**B** EXAMPLE: SUPPORT IN OLD AGE
COLLECTIVE INTEREST	**C** EXAMPLE: PUBLIC EDUCATION	**D** EXAMPLE: CONTRIBUTIONS TO SOCIAL SECURITY
SOCIAL INTEREST (total)	$E = A + C$	$F = B + D$

Figure 6.1 Costs and benefits of children.

forms. First, there are the contributions to social security and other taxes that will be paid when the children grow up and become part of the work force. A second type of benefit, more speculative, depends on the relation between the age structure of the population and innovation. Some analysts argue that young people are more likely to be innovators (thus the supply of innovations will grow faster) and that a growing population will create more demand for innovations because the markets are expanding. A growing population is also said to be good for organizations because they typically have pyramid-like hierarchical structures with more positions at the bottom than at the top. When a population is growing, the younger cohorts are larger than the older ones and this fits in well with the structure of organizations. By contrast, when a population is declining, there are more older workers than younger ones, and this can exacerbate tensions between the generations. Finally, there are some who believe that national power and prestige depends on population size; they fear that a decline in the U.S. population will lead to a decline in Western society and Western values (Wattenberg 1987).

Over time the balance between private and collective benefits has shifted, with children now more likely to be a source of positive externalities. Probably the most important change has been the shift from private to collective benefits in old age. Given the present social security system which provides retirement benefits and Medicare, and given the mobility of the population, with children often living far from their elderly parents, the private benefits of children are relatively smaller (and the collective benefits larger) than they were in earlier eras.

On the cost side of the ledger, private costs have probably increased relative to collective costs because the mother's time has become more valuable (leading to an increase in purchased childcare), and expenditures for private education have grown somewhat. The proportion of elementary and secondary school pupils enrolled in private schools has not changed (approximately one in eight in 1960 and 1985), but in 1960 the enrollment was overwhelmingly in Catholic schools, whereas in 1985 Catholic schools accounted for only about half of private enrollment. Thus, expenditures for private education have increased appreciably because tuition at non-Catholic private schools is about double the tuition at Catholic schools (*Statistical Abstract* 1987).

Analysts such as Ben J. Wattenberg are convinced that the national interest requires higher fertility, and they advocate several pronatalist policy changes such as child allowances and subsidized childcare. These recommendations have been questioned on several grounds. Some critics note that recent levels of immigration more than make up for the shortfall below replacement-level fertility. The counterargument is that large-scale immigration poses substantial social and political problems.

Another line of criticism questions our ability to predict future fertility. Joel Cohen, a mathematical demographer at Rockefeller University, writes, "There is far too much uncertainty about fertility a generation ahead for a demographic projection to justify many actions Mr. Wattenberg presses for, whatever the merits of those actions on other grounds" (1987, p. 20). In *The Fear of Population Decline,* Michael Teitelbaum and Jay Winter also caution against reading too much into the current low fertility rates: "To watch and wait seems the best counsel in discussions of population questions over the next decade" (1985, p. 152).

These warnings are understandable; past efforts to predict fertility have often failed spectacularly. But we don't really have the option of not predicting. Every policy, including the policy of waiting, rests on some implicit forecast of future events. These forecasts depend critically on our understanding of current fertility behavior. It is useful, therefore, to consider various explanations that have been offered.

Why So Few Children?

Some of the reasons given for the low fertility of the 1970s and 1980s stress *cyclical* or temporary phenomena which are likely to be reversed, whereas others emphasize *long-term* forces which are not likely to change. I believe that the decline is also directly related to women's quest for economic equality.

Cyclical reasons. Some economists such as Richard Easterlin (1987) see the low fertility as primarily a cyclical phenomenon, albeit a long cycle. Since 1973, the baby boomers have grown up, entered the labor market, tried to find housing, and have made decisions about marriage and family. They often decided to postpone having children, to have only one or two, or to remain childless. The decision to postpone, itself, often leads to lower fertility for physiological reasons such as increased difficulty in conceiving or the development of medical problems that make pregnancy more risky. Postponement can also have other effects (such as permitting the woman to develop a successful career) that also lead to fewer births.

The economic circumstances facing young people in the late 1970s and early 1980s were discouraging to childbearing in several ways. First, the cohort was very large. This would have put pressure on young people seeking jobs and housing even if the economy had been normal. Second, the economy was growing very slowly. Between 1973 and 1986 real GNP per capita grew at an average rate of only 1.2 percent per annum, less than half the 2.6 percent rate during the thirteen years preceding 1973. The slow growth was felt particularly keenly by young people. Real wages of men 25–34 *fell* by 13 percent between 1970 and 1985. Men 35–44 suffered only a three percent decline, and at ages 45–54 and 55–64 men's real wages rose slightly. In addition, the rapid inflation of the 1970s was particularly harmful to young people, most of whom did not already own houses or similar assets. If Easterlin's cyclical explanation is correct, fertility rates will rise when the cohorts born in the 1970s come to maturity in the 1990s and enjoy the benefits of their small numbers.

A different kind of explanation, also temporary or cyclical in nature, is based on the distinction between cohort fertility (the number of children ultimately born to women who were themselves born during a particular time period) and period fertility (the fertility rate during a particular period of time). According to some demographers, the low period fertility during the decade 1975–1985 is attributable at least in part to the baby boomers' *postponing* childbearing—not to a decrease in the number they will eventually bear (Teitelbaum and Winter 1985). If postponement is the explanation, once the average age of childbearing stops increasing (as it must), the period fertility rate will begin to rise.

Long-term factors. The long-term trend in fertility has been downward in the United States throughout the nation's history. Between 1800 and 1910 the rate fell by more than half, and between 1910 and 1980 it again fell by half. This trend, which has its counterpart in all economically developed countries, has been explained by economic changes such as a decrease in the benefits of children to parents, an increase in the costs of children, and improvements in birth control. (The decline in infant and child mortality also contributed to lower fertility by reducing the number of births needed to ensure the survival of any given number of children to adulthood.) In agricultural societies children can contribute to production at an early age. Moreover, in the absence of banks, insurance companies, and other financial institutions, children are desired by parents as a means of providing for their old age. With industrialization and urbanization, these benefits decrease, while the costs of raising children rise because of higher prices for housing and food. One of the biggest costs, the value of the mother's time, also rises as opportunities for paid work increase.

These changing costs and benefits suggest that, other things held constant, parents who deliberately calculate their optimal family size would want to have fewer children now than fifty or a hundred years ago. In addition, historical demographer Sheila Johansson argues that a long-term trend toward more deliberate decision making aimed at enhancing one's own welfare provides an additional explanation for low fertility: "As long as *rationality* . . . dominates the production of children, a rational population . . . is not likely to be able to perpetuate itself in the long run" (1987, p. 454). Johansson asks a highly provocative question:

"Why should risk-sensitive and/or cost-sensitive couples who find that a relatively inexpensive dog or cat can securely satisfy the urge for love, companionship, and nurturing inclinations have even one, let alone two or more, human children who may well disappoint or even reject their parents despite the large amount of money spent on their behalf?" (1987, p. 444).

Recent behavior of Americans provides some support for this view. According to the Pet Food Institute, there are approximately 106 million dogs and cats in the United States—over 50 million of each. Pets are far more numerous than children under age 18 (63 million); on average there is more than one pet per household. During the 1980s the number of children has remained stable, but the pet population has been growing at 4 percent per annum. Many pets are owned by older adults, or adults with children, but many are in childless households with adults of childbearing age.

Divergent expectations. Does the fact that young Americans are choosing to have fewer children reflect the wishes of women primarily, or of men? The logical answer is "both," but this answer must be understood in the context of women's quest for economic equality. Not only are men and women demanding fewer children for the cyclical and long-term reasons explained above, but I believe that their inability to agree on the terms of marriage and parental responsibility provides an additional explanation for low fertility. There are undoubtedly many childless men who would like to be fathers, but only under terms and conditions that women find unacceptable. There are undoubtedly many women who want to have children (or more children), but not if they must play a subservient role in a hierarchical marriage.

The mismatch between the wishes and expectations of many women and men helps to keep the birthrate low. The most difficult question to answer is whether this incongruity is a temporary phenomenon or one that is likely to persist. The optimists in the women's movement believe it is just a matter of time and socialization; a new generation of men will come along who will sympathize with women's desire for equality and who will accept a redefined role as husband and father. A survey of teenagers (Louis Harris 1987) reports that high school boys indicate a greater willingness to share domestic chores when they are married; whether their behavior will actually change remains unknown.

The evidence on this point from other countries is not reassuring. In the first flush of the Communist revolution, the Soviet Union tried to terminate patriarchy but "the Soviet experiment failed and was abandoned" (Millett 1970, p. 168). A joint U.S.-Soviet study in 1986 found that although Russian women are much more likely than American women to have a paid job, they get no more help at home from men than do women in the United States (Brozan 1987). In Jackson, Michigan, 55 percent of the women surveyed were in the labor force, while in the comparison city of Pskor in the USSR the participation rate was 81 percent. In both cities women spent twenty-five hours per week in housework and family care while men contributed only eleven hours.

In Sweden the government and the media have given robust support to women's desire for equality, but men's interests and attitudes have not changed accordingly. A lecturer on child psychology at the University of Stockholm, Lars Jalmert, complains that when he gives public talks on the role of the male parent, 85 to 90 percent of the audience are women (*Sweden Now* 1986).

Is the low fertility of the 1980s a temporary phenomenon? All things considered, the likelihood of a large, sustained upsurge in fertility in the United States is not great. The cyclical forces will probably change. The smaller cohorts reaching maturity in the 1990s are not likely to experience as much pressure in housing and job markets as young adults did in the late 1970s and early 1980s, and they may, as a result, marry earlier and have more children. It is also likely that some of the baby boomers' postponed births will be realized. The long-term forces leading to low fertility, however, will persist. Also, further improvements in birth control will contribute to holding down fertility by eliminating or sharply reducing unwanted births. Most important, women's desire to eliminate economic and social inequalities is likely to continue. How to reconcile that desire with the need for a population to reproduce itself constitutes a major social challenge.

The Care and Well-Being of Children

The issues surrounding the care and well-being of children are even more complex and more controversial than those concerning fertility. There are the "view with alarm" observers and those who think that things are not all that bad. When problems are identified, there are those who believe they are society's responsibilty, while other say that the parents are to blame. In sorting our way through this thicket of controversies and in seeking to draw inferences for policy, it is essential to distinguish between facts that are known with great confidence, inferences drawn from theory and empirical research that seem reasonable but not known with certainty, and speculations about causal relationships.

Facts about Children

There are a large number of well-established facts about children that indicate a deterioration in their well-being over the past few decades. Performance on scholastic aptitude tests declined markedly in the 1960s and 1970s, childhood obesity rose, and the incidence of poverty among children increased at the same time that it was falling for adults. Perhaps most significant of all (because it reflects young Americans' own assessment of their situation), the suicide rate at ages 15–19 in the early 1980s was two and one-half times as high as it was twenty years earlier.

Scholastic achievement. It is not easy to assess the scholastic performance of children, but almost all experts agree that the remarkable decline in scores on both the verbal and mathematical parts of the Scholastic Aptitude Test between the early 1960s and the late 1970s (see Figure 6.2) reflects a real decrease in intellectual achievement of American children, not just a change in the proportion taking the tests (College Entrance Examination Board 1977). Scores declined in all types of schools, among all socioeconomic groups, and in all parts of the country. The decline was almost twice as large for the verbal as for the mathematical scores. Test results leveled off and then rose slightly in the 1980s.

Attempts to explain the decline as the result of an increase in the proportion of high school students who take the SATs do not stand up to critical analysis. Average scores still show significant declines after adjustment for the composition of test takers, and the *absolute* number of students with high scores has declined

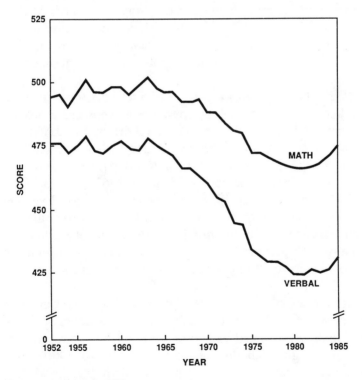

Figure 6.2 Average SAT scores.

markedly. In 1966–1967 more than 33,000 students had scores of 700 or above on the verbal portion, compared with fewer than 14,000 in 1986–1987 (Cahn 1987). This decrease occurred despite a jump from 1.4 to 1.8 million in the number taking the test.

It's not just the decline in number of high achievers that provides cause for concern. In 1987 four New York City banks, working with a coalition of churches, pledged to hire 250 graduates from five of the troubled high schools in the city. The standards that they set did not seem unduly rigorous: a high school diploma, no more than five unexcused absences in the senior year, and the ability to pass the equivalent of an eighth grade mathematics test. Fewer than 300 took the test or were interviewed, and the banks found that they could hire only 100 (Perlez 1987). Also in 1987 the New York Telephone Company gave its simple fifty-minute exam in basic reading and reasoning skills to 21,000 applicants for entry-level jobs. Only 16 percent passed (Simpson 1987).

Obesity. Obesity, a major nutritional disorder among American children, raises the risk of hypertension, psychosocial problems, respiratory disease, diabetes, and several orthopedic conditions. It is, therefore, disturbing that a detailed analysis of several national health examination surveys finds children were much more likely to be obese in the late 1970s than in 1963–1965 or 1967–1970 (Gortmaker et al. 1987). Among children 6 to 11 years of age, the proportion obese jumped from 18 to 27 percent in fourteen years while the proportion found to be superobese doubled, from 6 to 12 percent. In only ten years obesity among children 12 to 17 years rose from 16 to 22 percent, and superobesity from 6 to 9 percent.

These changes were all highly significant. Each survey involved thousands of children, with obesity carefully measured by triceps skin folds, an accepted diagnostic criterion that correlates well with the weight of children of given height and age. Obesity and superobesity increased more for black children than for white at all ages. The increase was greater for boys than for girls (both black and white) at ages 6–11, but greater for girls than for boys at ages 12–17. Most notable was an increase in superobesity among adolescent girls from 6 to 11 percent between the late 1960s and late 1970s.

Children in poverty. The proportion of children living in poverty is almost double that of adults: 20 percent versus 11 percent in 1986. This is an extraordinary situation; in 1960 and 1970 the poverty rate for children was only one-third above that of adults. Poverty status, it should be recalled, is determined by household income; all children and adults in any household are either in or out of poverty together. Why, then, is the rate for children so much larger than for adults?

The answer is to be found in variation in the number of children across households and the relation between this variation and the distribution of household income. If every household had the same number of adults and the same number of children, there could be no difference between children and adults in the incidence of poverty. In fact, the distribution is very uneven. Most adults (57 percent) live in households with no children, and only 9 percent of adults (but 40 percent of all children) live in households with three or more children.

Even if the number of children per household varied, there would be no difference in poverty rates if the households with more children had proportionately more income. However, the relative income of childless households has tended to rise (principally because of the improved position of the elderly), while the relative income of households with numerous children has tended to fall. For instance, average household income in households with four children was 8 percent *below* the mean household income in 1986, whereas it was 12 percent above the mean in 1970 and five percent above in 1960.

The poverty rate for children varies enormously, depending upon the type of household in which they live. Those fortunate enough to live with married parents are only slightly more likely to be in poverty than adults in general. By contrast, children who live in households without an adult male are extremely likely to

108 No One Is an Island

be in poverty. Unfortunately, the proportion of children living in such households almost tripled between 1960 and 1986, while the proportion living with a married coupled dropped from 90 to 76 percent.

Type of household	Poverty rate for children 1986		Distribution of children 1986	
	White	Black	White	Black
Married couple	11	19	80	45
No man present	51	70	12	40
Other	17	37	8	15
All	17	42	100	100

There is a huge difference in the poverty rate for black children compared to white; about half of this gap is accounted for by the race difference in distribution of children by type of household. The lower income of black men (compared to white men) and the larger number of children per household in black households also contribute to the gap.

Regardless of race or type of household, there has been a fall in the income available to children since 1980 because households with children are highly dependent on *labor* income, which did not grow in real terms. An increase in income inequality across households since 1980 has also hurt children more than adults (Fuchs 1986c).

Suicide. The most striking evidence of a worsening situation for young people during the 1960s and 1970s is the rise in suicide at ages 15–19 and 20–24 (see Figure 6.3). As is true of the decline in SAT scores, the growth of adolescent suicide is a real phenomenon, not to be explained away by changes in definitions or other vagaries of statistical reporting. The average of suicide rates among prime-age adults (25–64) was stable during those same decades.

Some observers try to minimize the importance of the higher suicide rate among youths by noting that there are "only" 5,000 such deaths each year. This reaction seems inappropriate for at least two reasons. First, each of these deaths usually has a demoralizing effect on many others—parents, grandparents, siblings, friends, fellow students, and often the entire community. Second, the actual suicides are only the tip of an iceberg, only the extreme expression of emotional problems present among a much larger number of young people who have attempted suicide, who are committing suicide slowly through substance abuse, or who engage in violent behavior that harms themselves and others.

Other indicators. Several other measures, albeit not as reliable as those just discussed because reporting may have changed, also

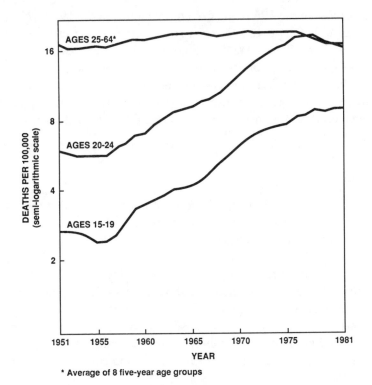

* Average of 8 five-year age groups

Figure 6.3 Suicide rates, by age (smoothed with three-year moving average).

indicate worsening conditions for children in recent decades. For example, the number of maltreatment cases reported per 10,000 children increased almost three-fold between 1976 and 1984 (*Statistical Abstract* 1987, p. 162). This could simply reflect better reporting, but no one is certain that this is the explanation. Marijuana use by junior and senior high school students rose in the 1970s, and children were starting at ever younger ages (Johnston et al. 1984, p. 96). Substance abuse among high school seniors appears to have fallen in 1987, but this may be, in part, a statistical artifact resulting from an increase in the dropout rate from high school.

The number of delinquency cases and dependency/neglect cases rose in the 1960s and even more rapidly in the 1970s (Nimick et al. 1982, pp. 8, 14). Again, the question of better reporting arises, but Michael Wald, a Stanford University law professor who specializes in problems of children, is convinced that there has been a significant increase in child neglect. He thinks the primary reasons are the abuse of alcohol and illegal drugs by parents, and the fragmentation of households (personal communication, December 11, 1987).

Causal Factors

When one turns from the question of *what* is happening to children to the question of *why,* the level of controversy rises. One frequently mentioned source of trouble is television. The national surveys of obesity showed a significant relation between the time spent watching television and the probability of a child's being obese (Dietz and Gortmaker 1985). At ages 12–17 the prevalence of obesity increased by 7 percentage points for each additional hour per day of television viewing. This association persisted even after controlling for prior obesity, race, socioeconomic class, and a variety of other family and environmental variables.

The role of television in the decline in SAT scores is subject to debate. Watching television often serves as a substitute for reading and writing, and this may explain why the decline in the verbal portion of the test was twice as large as in the mathematical portion. On the other hand, a Congressional Budget Office study concluded that television viewing "did not change in ways that would have contributed to the trends in test scores" (U.S. Congress 1987, p. xiii).

The role of television in delinquency, alcohol and drug use, and suicide is also unclear. Although one national study concluded that televised violence is a cause of aggression in children (National Institute of Mental Health 1982), television watching may be a symptom more than a basic cause. If it is used as a substitute for parental attention, or if children watch television because there aren't enough programs and facilities available to them for intellectual or physical activities, simply indicting television is not very helpful.

This brings us to the critical question of the possible adverse effects on children of a decline in care and supervision by parents, and the connection between this decline and women's quest for economic equality. My intent in raising this question is not to allocate blame. If children are in trouble it would be unfair to blame women more than men, but it would be irresponsible not to acknowledge the trouble or to try to understand its causes.

There is no doubt that the parental time potentially available to children fell appreciably between 1960 and 1986. On average, in white households with children there were ten hours less per week of potential parental time (total time minus time in paid work), while the decrease for black households with children was even greater, approximately twelve hours per week (these calculations are based on 1960 Census and March 1986 CPS tapes). When children were grouped by education of their mother, the greatest decline was among those whose mother had sixteen or more years of schooling. The principal reason for the decline was an increase in the proportion of mothers holding paid jobs, but the increase in one-parent households was also important, especially for black children.

It is theoretically possible that the potential parenting hours lost by mothers taking on paid jobs was offset by fathers providing more childcare, but this seems unlikely. Fathers hardly reduced their paid hours of work at all; thus, any increase in paternal childcare would have had to come out of the father's leisure or reductions in other work around the house. A national survey published in 1987 concluded, "Fathers are still not participating much in household maintenance or childrearing. Mother is still ultimately responsible for the custodial care of children. This was true even when a woman was working full time. Nor were younger men more likely to actively participate in childrearing than older men" (Genevie and Margolies 1987).

In place of parental time, there has been a substantial increase in other kinds of childcare arrangements. A large national survey ("Who's Minding the Kids" 1987) described these arrangements using the terminology "children of working women." This phrasing, which is quite common, implies that it is the woman's responsibility to arrange for childcare. This is an example of sex bias, but undoubtedly realistic as a description of actual practice. Most of these children, after all, could also be described as "children of working men."

According to the report, the home of a nonrelative is the most frequent arrangement for children under 5 years of age. Significantly, this is the type of care which most often breaks down and forces employed mothers to lose time from work. Other important sources of care include daycare centers, nursery schools, fathers, and the homes of grandparents. About 20 percent of school-aged children (ages 5–15) are reported as caring for themselves after school. The report states that this may underestimate the actual number of so-called latchkey children. A state commission on childcare in New York estimated that in that state alone approximately one million preschool and school-age children needed supplementary care during hours when parents or other responsible household members were out of the home (*New York Times,* January 4, 1987, p. 19). In California, a new program is said to serve "only 14,000 of the state's estimated 800,000 latchkey children" (Reinhold 1987).

The plight of the latchkey child comes through in a book entitled *A Friend for Frances* (Wills and Cook 1983), written for children ages 4–8. When the story opens, Frances, a third grader, is getting ready for her first day at a new school. She is quite apprehensive. Her mother helps her at breakfast and offers to drive her to school, but Frances declines and says she will take the school bus. The day does not go very well for Frances. Although the Care Bears try to help her, she does not make any friends. When school is over she comes home, makes a snack for herself, and goes out to the yard. Her mother is not in evidence, nor is any other adult or child. Suddenly, Tender Heart Bear appears, encourages her, and the following day she does make a friend.

The book is realistic in its avoidance of the stereotypical family of an earlier generation. There is no father in evidence in the household, Frances seems to be an only child, and she is obviously alone when she comes home from school. This is a situation which many children face. The unrealistic part is reliance on the Care Bears as the source of advice and emotional support.

How much or whether changes in childcare arrangements have contributed to the physical, mental, and intellectual problems of children is hard to assess. In *Children without Childhood,* Marie Winn (1983) is very critical of parents who have withdrawn "their close protective attention from children" as a result of divorce or the rise of two-career families. The loss of a father, either through divorce or death, has been a significant predictor of suicide (Paffenbarger et al. 1969), and a study of 102 teenagers who attempted suicide reported that only one-third lived with both parents (*Newsweek* 1978). Other observers, however, argue that children who are on their own become more independent and develop skills for coping with a difficult environment.

It has not been shown conclusively that the adverse trends in adolescent well-being are the result of reduced parental attention. Uhlenberg and Eggebeen (1986) believe that they are, and they offer as evidence the fact that these trends were correlated with rising divorce rates and increasing labor force participation by mothers of young children between 1960 and 1980. On the other hand, Furstenberg and Condran (1988), after a more detailed review of the relevant data both in the United States and abroad, reject that explanation, but do not propose an alternative of their own.

With respect to achievement in school, there is also considerable disagreement as to whether the mother's marital or employment status has any effect (see Myers et al. 1983, for a review of the relevant literature). When socioeconomic variables are *not* controlled for, within-school comparisons of children from one-parent and two-parent homes usually show the former as performing worse by almost every criterion (*Principal* 1980). This is not surprising because divorce, or birth to an unwed mother, almost always hurts children economically even if it does not have other harmful effects. The differential in school performance tends to disappear when income and parents' education are held constant. Within two-parent families, full-time employment by mother and father does seem to have a small negative effect on school performance of children, but in one-parent black families the children of employed mothers score higher than those with mothers without paid jobs (Myers et al. 1983).

Much of the research is cross-sectional—that is, it looks at children at a given point in time and tries to relate their performance in school to other variables measured at that same time. This methodology is problematic because many of the key variables, such as the mother's marital and employment status and family income, may change substantially over time. Children's performance in school is presumably affected by their entire previous experience, not just the immediate situation. One longitudinal study that combined data on parents' use of time in 1975–76 (when preschool children were present) with teacher ratings of those children in 1981–82 found that the mother's full-time employment had a significant negative effect (Stafford 1987). This study, however, was based on only seventy-seven children, and can hardly be considered definitive.

Policy Implications

Supposing that the trends set in motion by women's quest for economic equality have had harmful effects on children, what inferences should be drawn? There is no case for blaming women any more than men. To insist that women continue to accept second-class status is unfair. Furthermore, it seems unlikely that women will abandon their quest, or that fathers will, on average, supply the missing parental input (though there may be significant efforts by some men). Once we recognize the *legitimacy* of women's quest for economic equality, the problems of children become everyone's concern. Even adults who have no children need to be involved because the country's future depends on the physical and mental health of the next generation. Furthermore, the care of children and the fertility issue are intimately connected. Unless parents can afford and agree on good childcare arrangements, they are less likely to want children—and this anti-fertility effect will be greatest among those who feel most strongly about the need for satisfactory childcare.

Just as low fertility is seen as a temporary phenomenon by some analysts, it is possible that the problems experienced by children born in the 1960s and early 1970s will not be evident in more recent cohorts. Suicide rates rose and SAT scores fell during a period of social dislocation, with gender roles changing rapidly and in unexpected ways. Children caught in the midst of familial and social transitions may well have suffered more than those born later when new living patterns were more firmly established. Furthermore, the children born around 1960 frequently were late additions to large families. About 30 percent of births in 1960 were fourth-order or higher, and only 25 percent were first births. By contrast, of the children born in the late 1970s and early 1980s, only about 10 percent were fourth-order or higher, and more than 40 percent were first births. These children may have received proportionately more attention from parents and others.

This more optimistic view must remain conjecture at this point; almost all the relevant indicators are based on children born prior to 1975. We do not now know whether the cohorts born in the 1980s will, when they are teenagers, have suicide rates and school test scores at current levels or at the more favorable ones that prevailed in 1960. The one reliable measure available for children born in the 1980s is the poverty rate—and this is not reassuring. The poverty rate for children under age 6 in 1986 was 22 percent, up from 18 percent in 1980 and 17 percent in 1970. If very low income impedes children's physical, mental, and emotional development, the prospects for the most recent cohorts are not bright.

In summary, all Americans have a stake in the fertility rate and in the care of children. To the extent that these issues are related to women's quest for economic equality, all Americans have a stake in that issue as well. The desire for children and concern about their welfare contributes significantly to women's economic disadvantage. In the past, they could mitigate that disadvantage by accepting the constraints of a hierarchical marriage. Many still do. But the country as a whole is not likely to go back to the gender roles and relationships of an earlier era—better birth control and the opening up of jobs in a service economy preclude such a result. Society must deal with the world as it is today. What kind of message do we want to send? Do we want to encourage or discourage women from having children? Do we want these children to be well taken care of? We must decide on national priorities, and then choose policies to achieve those goals.

Chapter 7

What Can Be Done?

When economic well-being is measured comprehensively, women are worse off than men and, as a group, have made no gains relative to men since 1960. *Can* anything be done to reduce the inequality? Of course! Women's relative position is not a physical constant, like the force of gravity. It can be modified by human intervention, with measures as simple as having the U.S. Treasury send a monthly check to every woman or as complicated as having national wage boards raise the wage level in female-dominated jobs. *Should* anything be done? The case for public policy to help women in their quest for economic equality must rest on considerations of equity or efficiency or both. Equity refers to the fairness of the distribution of economic well-being. Efficiency refers to the allocation of resources to maximize the social good, given the distribution of income and abilities.

The data show that women are worse off than men; thus, people who favor a more egalitarian society can argue that equity requires some redistribution of economic rewards and power from men to women. There are, however, virtually no policies that would affect all women or all men equally. The benefits and costs of different programs are likely to vary with marital status, number of children, employment status, and other factors. Thus, equity issues *within* each sex must also be considered when choosing among policies. The efficiency argument depends primarily on the existence of externalities with respect to fertility and childcare. If private decisions with respect to children—both their number and their care—are not socially optimal, some reallocation of resources is desirable. Policies that help women may induce this reallocation.

There are many policies that would help women, but very few that would do so without cost. Sometimes the cost would be simply a *transfer* of income from men to women, but most often there would be *real* costs as well. The vital distinction between transfer costs and real costs is often ignored in policy discussions. For instance, recommendations to subsidize childbearing through generous child allowances (as is done in Czechoslovakia and many other East European countries) have been characterized by Teitelbaum and Winter as being very costly. They write, "Adoption by high-wage Western countries of financial incentives for childbearing that are comparable in relative terms to those of Eastern Europe will be a very expensive proposition" (1985, p. 149). But the transfer of income from childless individuals to parents does not, in itself, represent any real cost to society. Real costs only enter through the effects that policies have on efficiency in the allocation of resources. Does output fall? Are workers, investors, or consumers induced to change their behavior in ways that reduce total economic well-being?

The distinction between transfer and real costs can be illustrated by looking at the effects of a national health insurance program. Suppose there were no health insurance; people paid for their own care directly at the rate of, say, $100 billion annually. Now suppose that the government introduced a tax-supported national health insurance plan that would pay everyone's health care bill. If nothing else changed, there would be a *transfer* of $100 billion from taxpayers to the users of medical care, but there would be no *real* cost, except for administration of the plan. If there were no change in behavior, the output and efficiency of the economy would remain unaltered.

But behavior probably would change. We know from both economic theory and empirical research that when people have medical insurance they tend to use more medical care than when they are not insured. The best available estimates suggest that the change from no insurance to full insurance might result in an increase in use of about 35 percent (Manning et al. 1987). This additional care would provide some benefit to patients, but not $35 billion worth. Because insurance eliminates the direct cost to the patient, he or she will consume additional care as long as it has any benefit, however small. As a first approximation, let's put the value of the additional care to patients at $18 billion. The $17 billion difference between that value and the value of those resources in their best alternative use (given by their market price of $35 billion) represents a real cost to society—that is, an efficiency loss arising from a misallocation of resources.

Some efficiency or real cost will also be incurred on the supply side as a result of the additional taxes needed to finance the program. If the taxes are imposed on capital income, people may respond by saving and investing less than they otherwise would. If labor income is taxed, some people may cut back on their work effort. No one knows exactly how large these reductions would be, but tax simulation studies suggest that the real cost of raising $135 billion might be about $25 billion. If so, the total real costs of the program would be $42 billion. The program could still be justified on efficiency grounds, however, if the social benefits of the additional medical care (the externalities) exceeded the private benefits by more than $42 billion.

These same considerations are relevant for nearly all the public policies that have been proposed to help women in their quest for economic equality. Parental leaves, wages based on comparable worth, subsidized childcare, and so on would all involve transfer costs (for example, from the childless to those with children, or from men to women). They would probably involve real costs as well because people would change their behavior in response to the new programs. The transfer costs per se do not raise any issue of efficiency; they can be judged purely on equity grounds. The real costs do raise issues of efficiency, but the programs may be justified anyway because the equity issues are deemed more important or because the programs create benefits for society as a whole (positive externalities) that offset the real costs. For example, more care for children might result in less juvenile crime or fewer births to unwed teenagers.

Policies to help women can take many forms. Tax laws could

be changed, social security rules could be modified, and discrimination in a variety of settings such as business clubs could be prohibited. The most important policy initiatives, however, usually fall into one of two categories: *labor market* interventions such as affirmative action and comparable worth legislation, or *child-centered* policies such as family allowances and subsidized childcare.

Labor Market Policies

Most past attempts to help women have focused on the labor market and have aimed at changing the behavior of employers through antidiscrimination and affirmative action legislation. Current proposals such as wage determination based on comparable worth also depend on the view that women's problems lie primarily in the prejudiced or exploitative behavior of employers. (Policies such as employer-subsidized childcare and parental leaves will be discussed below, along with other child-centered policies, rather than in the labor market context.) The evidence presented in Chapters 3, 4, and 5 suggests that this view is mistaken. Past interventions in the labor market appear to have provided very little benefit for most women; more forceful policies might provide greater benefits, but the other consequences of such interventions must be considered as well.

Antidiscrimination Legislation

Laws requiring equal pay for equal work and forbidding sex discrimination in employment have been in force since the early 1960s; additional legislation of this type is likely to have primarily symbolic value. Prior to enactment of the 1963 and 1964 legislation, there were frequent allegations of widespread wage discrimination. Everyone seemed to know of many instances where women and men were "working side by side and the women are making 40 percent less," but remarkably few successful suits were brought in subsequent decades. Theoretically, the absence of suits might indicate that employers changed their wage policies after 1964 to avoid prosecution. If they did, the wage gap should have shrunk, but it did not. The overall difference between women's and men's wages as well as the gap within individual Bureau of the Census occupations showed little change between 1960 and 1980.

More vigorous enforcement of existing laws is unobjectionable, but not likely to result in any significant change for women as a whole. Even the most vigorous enforcement would not materially alter occupational segregation or reduce the large gap between the wages of women and men within the same occupation. After a detailed study of wages in narrowly defined office jobs, economist Francine Blau concluded, "For the most part, earnings differentials by sex within occupations are primarily the result of differences in pay rates among firms rather than differences in pay rates within firms" (1977, p. 101).

The situation for blacks was quite different. Discrimination and legally enforced segregation were widespread prior to the legislation and judicial decisions of the early 1960s. Within a few years, major changes were observable in the occupations of blacks and in their wages relative to whites. Within fifteen years the wage gap between black and white women had been eliminated and the gap for men appreciably reduced. Not all of the improvement should be attributed to the antidiscrimination efforts, but racial disparities were more readily affected by such efforts because discrimination played a larger role in their creation. During the 1980s, when antidiscrimination efforts weakened, the narrowing of black-white differences slowed markedly, but women's wages began to draw closer to men's at the unprecedented rate of one percentage point per year. This narrowing of the gap had very little to do with enforcement of the antidiscrimination laws, and a great deal to do with women's shifting their priorities from families to careers.

Affirmative Action

Government pressure on firms to place more women in high-paying jobs might have more effect than the antidiscrimination laws, but such pressure can also have negative consequences. Where the primary reason for the absence of women in such jobs is prejudice, forcing such action can be good all around—good for the women involved, good for the firms, and good for other women who can aspire to advancement. But when the primary reasons lie elsewhere—for example, the inability or unwillingness of women to commit to long and unpredictable hours, the travel requirements, or other aspects of jobs that conflict with women's family aspirations and commitments—affirmative action will turn out to be largely "tokenism." It will help a few, but leave the majority of women unaffected. It may even hurt some women—those who would have achieved advancement in the absence of affirmative action. An unqualified man in a high post is treated as a mistake of the system, but when a woman is promoted simply to satisfy an affirmative action edict, truly qualified women suffer.

Comparable Worth

The persistence of large-scale occupational segregation and wage differentials after more than two decades of antidiscrimination and affirmative action efforts has led many advocates of economic equality for women to shift the emphasis to "equal pay for work of comparable worth." This concept, which has been hailed as a panacea by some but also decried as "looney tunes" by U.S. Civil Rights Commission chairman Clarence Pendleton, is simple in theory but extremely complicated in practice.

Everyone agrees that occupations in which most of the workers are women pay lower wages than occupations that are primarily male, holding constant the level of education. (Librarians, for example, earn no more per hour than firefighters, even though librarians have, on average, about three years more education.) Advocates of comparable worth say that jobs can be evaluated by objective standards such as educational requirements and degree of responsibility, and that firms should be forced to set wages according to those standards. Numerous lawsuits have been brought under this theory, and some state and local governments have adopted the comparable worth approach in principle. Neither the federal government nor any state has yet attempted to impose a comparable worth standard on the private sector, but that is the goal of many supporters of women's rights.

The critics and skeptics of comparable worth have rejected it on theoretical grounds, have pointed to practical difficulties in implementation, and have argued that it would do little to reduce economic inequality. The theoretical rejection comes from mainstream economists who claim that wages set by administrative rules (no matter how objectively determined) will be less efficient than wages determined by the interplay of demand and supply. A classic example of how comparable worth can interfere with the efficient allocation of resources is the problem of setting wages for an English-French translator and an English-Spanish translator in the same firm. (This example was given by Sharon Smith, in Gold 1983.) It is difficult to imagine a set of comparable worth criteria that would not result in approximately equal wages for the two jobs. It is, however, very easy to imagine that in particular markets the demand for, or supply of, English-Spanish translators might differ so much from the situation for English-French translators that competition would result in different wages for the two types of jobs. In those circumstances, insistence on equal wages would produce "surpluses" (of the translators whose wage was set above the competitive market level) and "shortages" (of those whose wage was set too low). Such surpluses and shortages on a wide scale throughout the economy would depress the efficiency and real output of the society.

A different type of theoretical criticism comes from a feminist perspective. For instance, economist Nancy Barrett (1982, pp. 164–165) worries that comparable worth would perpetuate gender differences in the work force (and at home). It would remove incentives for women to seek out better-paying "male" jobs and would encourage them to continue to work at jobs that are more compatible with housework and childcare.

Some critics stress the practical difficulties of implementing comparable worth. They note the problem of choosing which criteria to use in determining the value of a job—education? responsibility? working conditions? and so on—and the even greater problem of deciding how much weight to give each criterion. For instance, how much additional responsibility or how much noise on the job is equal to one additional year of schooling? Another practical problem is the difficulty of enforcing a comparable worth policy on firms with relatively few employees—firms that in the aggregate account for a large fraction of total female employment.

Most critiques of comparable worth do not have a quantitative base, but a detailed statistical analysis by Johnson and Solon (December 1986) is an important exception. They looked at the wages of a large sample (24,000 men and 19,000 women) of nonagricultural workers in 1978 and estimated how much of the wage gap between the sexes would disappear if the relationship between wages and the percent of an occupation that is female could be eliminated. They concluded that implementation of comparable worth by every employer might reduce the existing overall wage differential of 34 percent by 3 to 8 percentage points, depending upon assumptions concerning what criteria would or would not be considered in setting wages. They pointed out that implementation by every employer is unlikely; comparable worth rules are likely to be confined to the public sector and large private firms. In that case, the effect on the overall wage gap would be no greater than 3 and possibly less than 2 percentage points. The principal reason for the small effect is that comparable worth as usually proposed would affect disparities only *within* the same firm, whereas most of the sex gap in wages is *between industries* and *between firms* in the same industry.

These criticisms of comparable worth have merit, but need not be decisive. The economic theorists are undoubtedly correct that interference with market-determined prices will lead to some inefficiency and loss of output, but it is crucial to know *how much*. If the real costs are small, they may be outweighed by considerations of equity or by positive externalities flowing from effects on fertility and childcare. Barrett may be correct in saying that comparable worth will perpetuate sex segregation in occupations and unequal responsibility for housework and childcare, but such differences might be more acceptable to women if they earned more relative to men.

The practical difficulties of implementing comparable worth seem to be exaggerated. Most large firms already set wages for different jobs through evaluation procedures similar to those that have been proposed for comparable worth. Indeed, there are several large, highly successful consulting firms whose principal product is the creation of rating schemes for every job in an organization, from the chief executive officer down to the lowest-level entry position. The comparable worth advocates say that these systems could continue to serve as the basis for wage setting, with the alleged bias against female-dominated jobs removed.

Johnson and Solon are correct in maintaining that elimination of wage disparities between female and male jobs in individual firms will not have much effect on the overall wage gap, but most women would welcome a gain of even a few percentage points. Also, there could be a more universal system of administratively determined wages that operated across firms and industries as well as within firms.

In order to gain more understanding of the possible effects of comparable worth on employment, output, income, and economic efficiency, my colleagues and I developed a computable general equilibrium model of the U.S. economy that introduced such a universal system. (The economy can be simulated on a computer, and the results of policy interventions can be calculated.) Our policy intervention required equal pay for men and women of the same education regardless of job or industry (Beider et al. forthcoming).

Through simulations we estimated effects for the economy as a whole, for each production sector, and for individuals grouped by sex, marital status, and education. The model is only a rough approximation to the real world, but it taught us a great deal about comparable worth. The process of model construction forced us to consider issues such as the hiring rules that would probably have to accompany the wage rules, and the nature of decision making in married households. These issues have usually been ignored in theoretical discussions. The model also facilitated the investigation of the effects of comparable worth on employment and output after allowing for demand and supply responses to changes in relative wages and prices.

Every policy intervention changes the incentives and constraints facing some individuals, usually through shifts in prices and income. Policy analysis requires identification of which individuals—employers? workers? consumers?—are likely to be affected, and how. Economic theory indicates the likely direction of the effects, and empirical research suggests probable magnitudes. Finally, the policymaker must consider the *values* to be placed on the various effects. Whether a policy is good or not depends on an evaluation of all its consequences.

If women's wages are set equal to men's at equal levels of education (regardless of the jobs they hold), the following effects should be expected.

1. Employers would try to replace women workers with men or replace them with capital equipment. For instance, if typists' wages rose by 30 or 35 percent, firms would be tempted to cut back on typists and buy word processors for their mid-level managers. Note that this substitution would occur regardless of whether the previous disparity between women's and men's wages reflected difference in the value of the work to the firm (productivity) or prejudice against women (discrimination).

2. Higher wages for women would lead to more female labor force participation, especially by married women. Their participation rates would rise more dramatically than those of unmarried women because the latter are already at a higher level. Moreover, if women's wages rise 30–35 percent in current dollars while men's wages remain unchanged, there would be a substantial increase in the average price level, and thus a decrease in the

real wages of men. This decrease would result in a small decrease in men's labor force participation. Married men would probably be affected more than those not married because of the possibility of changing the allocation of market and nonmarket work between husband and wife in response to the change in relative wages.

3. Labor costs, and therefore prices, in industries that employ proportionately more women would rise relative to those which employ mostly men. Consumers would respond by purchasing less of the output of those industries with above-average price increases.

4. The efforts of employers in all industries to shift away from female employment, the shift in consumer demand away from female-intensive industries, and the increase in women's desire for paid work would lead to considerable unemployment of women. The employment of unmarried women would be particularly affected as they would face increased competition from the influx of married women into the labor market.

5. The elimination of the wage gap would, on average, raise women's economic well-being and lower men's. The increase in unemployment among women would be more than offset by their higher wages and increased leisure. The economy as a whole would operate somewhat less efficiently because of the reallocations of resources induced by the changes in relative wages and prices. If the original wage gap were the result of discrimination, the loss in efficiency from the reallocations would be relatively small, but if the gap reflected productivity differences between women and men the losses would be large.

6. The effects on economic well-being would vary greatly by marital status. Unmarried women would gain much more than married women because the latter's gains would be offset (at least in part) by the lower real income of their husbands. Depending on the sharing rules within households and on the relative hours of work and wages of husband and wife, many married women could experience an absolute decline in economic well-being as a

result of comparable worth. Married men, on the whole, would not fare as badly as single men because the former would get some benefit from their wives' higher wages.

7. In order to keep employers from substituting men for women, there would be pressure to impose hiring rules as well as wage rules. For instance, employers might be required to maintain their historical proportions of women and men. Alternatively, they might be required to employ women and men in proportion to qualified applicants. The empirical simulations show unequivocally that the efficiency losses for the economy as a whole would be much greater with a rule of historical proportions than with one based on applicant proportions.

8. If comparable worth were introduced in only part of the economy (say, government and large firms) the effects on the wage gap, employment, output, and efficiency would be smaller than if there were universal coverage. However, if the original wage gap were the result of discrimination (rather than productivity differences), the efficiency losses would be greater with partial than with universal coverage.

The simulations did not consider the possibility of evasion of comparable worth rules (possibly similar in effect to partial coverage) or the administrative and enforcement costs of a comparable worth wage system, nor did it allow employers to resort to greater reliance on "temporary" labor, more purchased inputs, or similar restructuring. These "quasi-legal" evasions would reduce the benefits of comparable worth to women.

The problems of transition to comparable worth could be considerable if it were introduced in many sectors at the same time. Wage parity between women and men requires a steep rise in women's wages or a steep fall in men's; the former approach is likely to be more feasible, but must result in inflation. Also, the shifts in relative wages and prices would be greater than those experienced when the Organization of Petroleum Exporting Countries (OPEC) raised the price of oil in 1973. Thus, the dynamic shock effects of the transition might be very large. In the long run, comparable worth might have substantial effects on marriage, divorce, fertility, and educational attainment; these factors were all held constant in the simulations.

The results of the simulations offer support both to those who oppose comparable worth because they expect it to have adverse effects on efficiency and real output, and to those who favor comparable worth because it would redistribute income from men to women.

Other Labor Market Policies

There are several other policies that could be imposed on employers or adopted voluntarily in order to help women. For instance, reduction of the official full-time work week to thirty hours would benefit those women who prefer to work fewer hours and might also cause employers to hire more women (rather than pay overtime rates to men). The failure of firms to voluntarily adopt thirty-hour weeks suggests that there would be real costs to such a policy—but these costs might be borne disproportionately by men. Thus, the policy could, on balance, help women.

Women's rights advocates frequently urge employers to offer more flexibility regarding hours of work, including shared jobs, part-time jobs, and flex time. These policies would obviously help women who have significant responsibilities at home. Why don't employers comply? There are two main possible explanations: First, employers may not realize that these innovations would be advantageous to them. By helping to meet the needs of their employees, especially the women in their work force, they would be able to attract and keep better personnel, have higher morale, and perhaps even higher productivity. A personnel officer of a worldwide electronics firm that is headquartered in California and operates many plants in that state told me that flex time (the right of workers to choose their own starting times within reasonable limits) is the cheapest and most effective fringe benefit the company offers. It is extremely popular with the workers and, so far as he can see, does not really cost the company anything.

In some situations, however, there may be a cost to the company to having part-time jobs or flex time or shared jobs. This cost may arise because of difficulties in scheduling and coordination, through additional costs per worker for space and fringe benefits, or because of poorer service to customers. If there is a cost associated with these arrangements, who should bear it? The cost could be spread over all workers, just as many of the fringe benefits a company offers are spread, rather than charged to the individual worker. Another possibility is that the cost be passed on to the consumer in the form of higher prices, and a third is that the cost be borne by the individuals who benefit from the new arrangements. A New England restaurant chain, for instance, advertised for help with the following offer: "Five dollars an hour if you choose the hours, or seven dollars an hour if we choose the hours."

It is good social policy to allow flexibility in these matters. Flex time and part-time jobs can help men and women deal more effectively with their parental obligations. We should be wary of legislation or other institutional barriers (such as union regulations) that keep employers and employees from making arrangements concerning hours and pay that are mutually beneficial.

Child-Centered Policies

In recent years preoccupation with labor market policies has diminished slightly and attention is shifting to child-centered policies that could help women in their quest for economic equality. These policies can take many forms: child allowances (or tax credits), subsidies for childcare, parental leaves, and so on. In appraising the effects of such policies, it is necessary to determine whose behavior will be affected and in what way. Different policies are likely to have different implications for efficiency and also likely to have different distributional consequences.

Policies that change the economic incentives and constraints facing individuals are analogous to changes in an ecological system. Ecologists know that even modest alterations in the natural environment, such as elimination of an insect or the introduction of a new species of plant, can set in motion a complex chain of reactions and interactions. So it is with alterations in the economic and social environment; policymakers need to be alert to all the possible consequences of their interventions. For example, consider the very modest child-centered policy enacted in California (and upheld by the U.S. Supreme Court in January 1987) that requires employers above a certain size to grant new mothers a four-month maternity leave without pay and to guarantee return to the old job if the woman so desires. It is instructive to analyze the diverse potential effects of even such a simple policy.

Parental Leave

First, it should be noted that some firms would offer such a benefit voluntarily, much as they might offer health insurance or pensions. It is a form of compensation that helps to attract workers. But what about employers who are forced to offer this benefit against their better judgment? How might they react?

1. They will probably be less willing to hire women who are likely to avail themselves of this benefit, or less willing to place such women in positions where the four-month interruption would present problems for the firm. A letter to the editor of *Savvy* (June 1987, p. 6) from a woman in New York City says, "Calling it parental leave doesn't change the reality; employers know which sex will take advantage of this leave and, consequently, which sex to avoid hiring because of it. The underlying message of mandated parental leave is that women aren't serious about doing serious work."

2. The policy will be more burdensome for smaller firms than for larger ones because of greater difficulty in juggling assignments and shifting personnel. Those firms that are small enough to escape the policy entirely have a disincentive to increase the size of their work force. *One* relatively minor policy of this sort is not likely to have a large effect on employers, but if there are several that only become operative (or are only enforced) for

firms above a certain size, we should expect firms that are just below that size to resist hiring additional employees. If demand for their output increases, they would try to make as much use as possible of purchased services, temporary help, and similar devices. These policy-induced distortions in behavior contribute to inefficiency in the economic system.

3. Industries and firms that employ a large percentage of women will be more affected than those that do not. Their prices will rise and demand will fall. For example, women ages 20–39 account for more than one-third of total employment in finance, insurance, real estate, and services, but only 5 percent in construction and only 8 percent in mining.

The parental leave policy also has implications for women's labor market behavior:

1. Employed women are more likely to take time off from work during the leave period.

2. Women are more likely to work prior to having a child because they can count on the leave.

3. Women are more likely to return to work after the end of their leave because the old job is guaranteed. It is possible, however, that the parental leave period would make them more attached to their child, in which case they might be less likely to return to work than if they had gone back very soon after giving birth.

4. Women (and some men) who expect to become parents will prefer employment in covered firms. Other women and most men will, other things equal, prefer working in uncovered firms to the extent that parental leaves impose costs on them.

5. Women who expect to give birth will have more incentive to strive for better jobs, knowing that their position will be held open for their return.

A parental leave policy could also affect fertility by encouraging employed women to have children. Potentially, some of the most important effects could be on the children themselves. The leave may allow a better bond to develop between the child and the mother during the first few months after birth. To the extent that the policy encourages women to return to paid work after four months, it increases the number of very young children who are cared for by others.

This list does not exhaust all the possible effects, but it is sufficiently comprehensive to show how complicated is the task of formulating public policy in a reasonable way. A policy is invoked to achieve a particular objective, but so long as individuals and firms are free to modify their behavior in light of the policy, there can be numerous effects in a variety of directions, not all of which are desired. From this perspective let us consider some of the more widely discussed child-centered policies.

Child Allowances

A cash grant from the government to mothers of young children is the most direct way of helping women via their children. Such grants can be structured in a variety of ways, depending upon the goals of the policymakers. For instance, grants could be limited to unwed mothers, as was true of Aid to Families with Dependent Children in some states. They could be limited to mothers with paid jobs, or they could be conditional on having low income. But programs that provide a benefit conditional on a characteristic that can be, at least in part, modified by the individual are problematic. People do respond to financial incentives. If policymakers want to encourage unwed motherhood or induce mothers to take paid jobs, they should structure the program accordingly; if they don't, they should consider broader conditions of eligibility. If the main purpose is to help women and children, the program should be as *neutral* as possible; that is, the grants should not discriminate against some women in favor of others and distort the choices that women make. Such distortions introduce inefficiencies and reduce the value of the grant.

Child allowances given to mothers without conditions would probably have a slight negative effect on their labor force participation because their need for earned income would be reduced. Similarly, it might have a slight negative effect on marriage because the woman would be less financially dependent on a man. On the other hand, the dowry-like aspects of child allowances could be an incentive to men to marry. The increase in women's viability outside marriage would strengthen their position within marriage, as explained in Chapter 4.

Child allowances would tend to increase fertility, but the effect would probably be small unless the allowances were structured primarily with a fertility objective. Countries that use child allowances to promote fertility usually give larger amounts for third and fourth children than for first and second births.

Probably the most difficult question about eligibility concerns household income. Should the allowances be the same for all income groups? Should they rise with income, or the reverse? A regressive pattern—that is, allowances that rise with family income—is implicit in plans that work through tax-deductibility. If families can deduct, say, $4,000 from taxable income for each child, the high-income family in the 30 percent tax bracket will save $1,200, but the lower-income family in the 15 percent bracket would save only $600.

A progressive pattern—one in which allowances fall as income rises—is preferred by those who want to use child allowances to achieve a more equitable distribution of income in general. This approach, however, has distortionary consequences. For instance, suppose a woman is eligible for a $4,000 allowance for her children if she makes only $10,000 per year, but the allowance falls to $2,000 if her income rises to $15,000 per year. Her effective tax on the extra $5,000 of earnings would be about 60 percent, because she loses $2,000 in benefits as well as paying about $1,000 in additional income tax and social security tax. This high marginal tax lowers her incentive to seek a better job or to work harder. Another disadvantage of varying the allowances inversely with income is that it distorts the pronatal effect toward low-income families.

If child allowances were given to mothers, women who are raising children alone would clearly benefit a great deal, but even married women would benefit to the extent that they would have more bargaining power within the household (the "proportionate" sharing model). An allowance of $2,000 per child under age 12 would require about $83 billion, equal to about 2.5 percent of total personal income. If a proportional tax were levied on all households except those in poverty, the net effect of the allowances and the tax would be an increase in the economic wellbeing of women relative to men of 2 percentage points (assuming an average of the equal and proportionate sharing models). For black women the increase would be 3 percentage points. The allowances would sharply reduce the proportion of children under 12 who are living in poverty—from 21 to 11 percent, assuming no change in behavior. There would undoubtedly be some adverse behavioral responses to the allowances and taxes and some administrative costs, but on balance such a program would clearly help women relative to men and would help children relative to adults. Moreover, even if the child allowances do not vary with household income and the tax is proportional to household income, the program would result in some redistribution from high- to low-income households.

Other Policies

Subsidized childcare is similar to child allowances in many ways, and many of the same observations concerning eligibility pertain. This form of help introduces another distortion, however: it benefits only those women who place their children in the care of others. If it is the intent of policymakers to discourage women from caring for their own children, subsidized care would be an appropriate choice; otherwise a child allowance would be preferable because it would allow those who want to buy care to do so while giving other women the option of providing care themselves.

Parental leaves are similar to subsidies for childcare in that they benefit only a subclass of mothers—in this case those who have paid jobs. Paid parental leave with pay geared to the parent's wage has the same regressive character as tax-deductibility: the value of the benefit rises with income.

Costs

The method of allocating the costs of child-centered policies requires careful attention. Probably the most fundamental distinction is between reliance on a broad-based tax such as the income tax, or methods that attempt to pin the costs on particular employers or particular industries. The economic perspective suggests that the broader approach will usually be more efficient and more equitable. Indeed, the whole idea of "employer-provided" benefits such as subsidized childcare is quite misleading. It leaves the impression that the costs will come out of the pockets of some nameless, faceless, high-paid executives. That is completely unrealistic. It is possible that the costs will be borne by the owners of the firm and show up in reductions in dividend payments, or, if losses ensue, in failure to meet the interest and repayment obligations on fixed debt. But this is not the most probable outcome. In all but the least competitive circumstances, the costs of childcare subsidies or other benefits will be translated into higher prices for the firms' output and/or lower wages for workers in those firms.

To say that costs imposed on employers will be transferred to investors, workers, and consumers is not to say that this is a bad policy, but it should force one to stop and ask whether this is the most efficient and equitable way of collectivizing the costs. Funding child-centered programs through the income tax or other broad-based taxes is not free of problems either, but usually introduces less inequity and inefficiency into the economic system than policies that distribute costs in a relatively arbitrary and selective way.

If the potential utilization of childcare services were more or less equal across industries, the distinction between a broad-based tax and one focused on employers would not be critical. But the relative importance of employed women with a child under age 6 is very uneven across firms and industries. In apparel manufacturing, for instance, mothers of young children constitute 15 percent of the work force, but in firms manufacturing durable goods they account for only 4 percent, and in mining and construction less than 2 percent. Thus, mandating employers to provide childcare is equivalent to imposing a tax whose rate varies widely from industry to industry and firm to firm. It would be much fairer, and less disruptive to economic efficiency, to impose an equal tax on all employers.

The "Iron Law of Childcare"

The call for "affordable, quality care for all children" stands high on the agenda of almost all groups seeking to improve women's economic position. Because it is so difficult for them to afford good, dependable childcare, many women are kept out of the labor market or find that their choice of jobs is limited by the constraints imposed by their childcare arrangements. Women who do not wish to make such career sacrifices often remain childless.

Complaints about the high cost of childcare stand in contrast to another oft-heard argument—namely that the providers of childcare are "underpaid." It is often said that "society does not put sufficient value on childcare and therefore underpays those who provide it."

There is substantial evidence to support both types of complaint. Women "childcare workers" earn only about two-thirds as much per hour as other women at comparable levels of education. (In calculating this figure, I excluded women who worked fewer than twenty hours per week and excluded all childcare workers employed in private households regardless of hours of work.) On the other hand, the average charge for one child in a daycare center in 1987 was around $100 for a full week. "Family" daycare (paid care in someone else's home) is usually less expensive than care in a center; but the cost of a caregiver in the child's own home is usually the most expensive form.

Because childcare is a labor-intensive activity, the cost of care and the wage of the caregiver are inextricably related; I call this the "iron law of childcare." The only way to reduce the cost is to lower the wage or to increase the number of children per caregiver. Either approach jeopardizes the quality of care.

Consider the financial situation of a well-organized childcare center. Its costs fall into two approximately equal parts: (1) the wages of the caregivers; and (2) fringe benefits, supervision, insurance, rent, equipment, supplies, electricity, and other operating expenses. Thus, the cost per hour of childcare is approximately twice the hourly wage of the caregiver divided by the number of children per caregiver.

For most working women with two preschoolers who need care, the cost is prohibitive. For example, suppose a woman earns the same wage as the caregiver, let's say $8.00 per hour. Assume the childcare center has one caregiver for every six children. The cost per hour per child would be $2.66 ($2 \times 8 \div 6$), and two children would cost $5.32. This would almost equal the mother's take-home pay after deductions for income and social security taxes. The cost must be paid—if not by the parents, then by someone else. The favorite candidate seems to be the employer, but this is illusory for the reasons explained above.

In summary, all proposals to help women, through labor market interventions, child-centered policies, or other ways, need to be appraised in light of efficiency (what are the real costs and benefits?) and distributional equity (who bears the costs and who receives the benefits?). In addition, different policies are likely to have different effects on a wide range of social issues, including freedom of choice, fertility, the care of children, and the extent of sex-role differentiation. These effects must be appraised in the light of one's own values.

Chapter 8

Conclusion

We live in a time of enormous stress, resulting partly from revolutionary changes in gender roles and relationships. I hope that this book has provided an understanding of the nature of these changes and the reasons for them. I also hope that it will foster clear and compassionate thinking about the difficult choices we face in our personal lives and as a society in coming to terms with women's quest for economic equality. I have examined the causes and consequences of the sex-role revolution of the past quarter-century, have noted the persistence of major differences between women and men in the labor market and at home, and have attempted to explain these differences. In addition, the case for policies aimed at helping women was presented, and the likely effects of such policies were considered.

Despite major antidiscrimination legislation and a quarter-century of revolutionary social change, women as a group have not improved their economic well-being relative to men. Unmarried white women who are young and well educated are the only significant exception to this conclusion. Women's economic disadvantage is usually attributed to employer discrimination, but this explanation falters on two counts. First, the supporting evidence is weak; and second, there are a large number of hard facts that are inconsistent with it.

The evidence in support consists partly of the discrimination cases brought and won since the early 1960s, plus anecdotal material. The remarkable point, however, is not that there were and probably still are such cases and such anecdotes, but how few of them have surfaced (relative to total female employment) since 1963. Also remarkable (like the failure of the dog to bark in the Sherlock Holmes story) is how little impact the antidiscrimination legislation of the early 1960s has had on trends in women's employment, occupational segregation, and the wage gap. If prejudice and exploitation had been pervasive prior to 1963, the new laws should have made a bigger difference.

The second type of evidence that is invoked in support of the employer hypothesis is the inability of researchers to explain statistically all of the wage gap by sex differences in schooling, work experience, and other socioeconomic factors. The unexplained portion of their regression analysis is labeled "discrimination," but this conclusion is suspect. It is analogous to concluding that physicians discriminate against men because statistical analyses leave unexplained a substantial sex difference in life expectancy.

The facts that are difficult to reconcile with the employer hypothesis were spelled out in detail in Chapters 3 and 4. They include the pattern of occupational segregation, the extensive segregation by industry, and several extraordinary features of women's wages, features that are the same in the late 1980s as they were in 1960. It is not employers who cause the wages of married women relative to those of unmarried women to fall 20 percent as the women age from 25 to 40. It is not employers who cause the wages of mothers in their thirties to lag (relative to childless women) by from 7 to 10 percent for each additional child. It is not employers who are responsible for the more than 40 percent gap in hourly earnings of *self-employed* women relative to self-employed men. And it is not employers who impose the limitations on hours of work, location, and travel that keep so many women with families from obtaining better-paying jobs.

Discrimination against women undoubtedly persists, not only in the labor market but in most economic and social institutions. But the biggest source of women's economic disadvantage—namely, their greater desire for and concern about children—is more fundamental, though it is impossible to say how much results from "nature" and how much from "nurture." Women's stronger commitment to parenting can be inferred not only from statistical studies but also from a wide variety of other sources, ranging from literary works to the clinical experience of psychotherapists. Motherhood and fatherhood are not symmetrical, are not simply opposite sides of the same coin. Both are strongly influenced by socialization—but in the case of fathers, socialization is practically the whole story. Motherhood is different. Women make a huge investment in pregnancy, childbearing, and nursing—an investment that is crucial to the perpetuation of the species. The father's investment, in terms of time and energy, is usually much smaller. Unlike other male primates, human fathers did become involved with their children, but typically in a patriarchal, hierarchical context. How to preserve that involvement in an egalitarian context is one of the great challenges facing modern society.

Scenarios for the Future

All revolutions end, some quietly and some with a roar. Some trigger counterrevolutions, while others provide launching pads for further change. What does the future hold for the sex-role revolution? It was, in part, one manifestation of the broader egalitarian ethos of the 1960s and 1970s, an ethos that has been arrested and reversed in the anti-egalitarian atmosphere of the 1980s. But the roots of the revolution go deeper than that.

If women's quest for economic equality were motivated only by the "spirit of the sixties," it too would have weakened in the 1980s, but it did not. In fact, on the wage front, women have made major gains in recent years after several decades of relative stability. The narrowing of the wage gap, however, has been accompanied by trends with respect to family and leisure that many, although not all, women find adverse. Most women say that they would like to be married, but an ever-increasing proportion are not. Most women say they want to be mothers, but an increasing proportion are childless and many of those who have children find that mothering requires major sacrifices in careers and leisure time.

In short, it is a time of conflicting trends, and predictions about the future are particularly hazardous. But such predictions must be made. It is impossible to make choices without some notion, explicit or implicit, as to what the future will be. This section describes four possible scenarios and considers the probability of their realization.

Return to Tradition

There are many Americans who hope that the country will return to the gender roles and relationships that prevailed prior to 1960. This means, first and foremost, that women would specialize in the roles of wife and mother, and that men would specialize in paid work. Marriage would be more universal than it is now, and much less subject to termination by divorce. Fertility would be substantially above current levels.

This scenario is not impossible. In the short run there may be some movement in this direction for reasons emphasized by Richard Easterlin (1987). The smaller cohorts born in the 1970s (only 3.2 million births per year in 1971–1975, versus 4.1 million ten years earlier) will face less competition in labor and housing markets, and their sense of economic ease may lead to earlier marriages and more births. Fear of AIDS (Acquired Immune Deficiency Syndrome) is currently inducing a return to more traditional lifestyles. Over a longer period, traditional roles might be reinforced by war, or by a "state of siege" mentality (as they have been, to some extent, in Israel). But absent some dramatic discontinuity in political and social conditions, a "return to tradition" that lasts for several decades seems unlikely. The roots of the sex-role revolution are primarily economic and technologic, and these forces continue to pull young people away from traditional roles.

A Split Society

A return to tradition by all or most of the population is unlikely, but there is a greater possibility that society may become deeply divided between an "orthodox religious" minority and a "secular modern" majority. The former group, constituting perhaps one-fourth the population, would include Mormons, orthodox Jews, staunch Catholics, fundamentalist Protestants, and others with deep religious convictions that shape their behavior with respect to marriage, children, and work. Fertility in this group would be high—an average of three or four children per woman. Some of the women, perhaps many, would also have paid jobs, but family would be their first priority.

By contrast, fertility in the majority of the population would be low, averaging no more than one or one-and-one-half children per woman. In this "secular modern" group, paid work would be almost as important for women as for men. Some men and women would marry; many would not. Those who did marry or live together without marriage would rely heavily on purchased goods and services for support of domestic life, with men and women sharing responsibility for the rest much more equally than in the 1980s.

On the reasonable assumption that the pull of modernity would result in net migration from the "orthodox religious" to the "secular modern," this split society could be demographically stable for a long period. For example, suppose the first group constituted one-fourth of the population and had four children per woman while the other group had, on average, one-and-one-third children per woman. Average fertility for the country as a whole would be two per woman, which is very close to the rate necessary for a stationary population in the long run. There would, no doubt, be some switching of individuals in each direction, but if the net outflow from the "orthodox religious" in each generation were one-half, the split in society would be maintained in constant proportion, and the process could go on indefinitely. If, however, the net outflow were less than one-half, the higher fertility of the "orthodox religious" would give them an ever-increasing share of the population; if it were more than one-half, their share would diminish.

A "split society" seems more probable than a return to tradition, but even if demographically stable, it might not be politically viable. Would the tensions and conflicts between the two groups with respect to public and private policies grow so great as to plunge the country into civil disorder? Or would an effective compromise be reached? The outcome of the abortion controversy may provide a partial answer to this question.

Egalitarian Stability

Many leaders of the women's movement dream of a society in which there would be equality in the labor market and in the home: all careers would be open to women, and men would do half the housework and childcare. This scenario is still far from realization and its chances are not great even over the next one or two generations. Beyond that point, new biomedical technologies and other changes that are currently envisioned only in science fiction may radically alter the relevance of gender. For instance, John Varley (1980, 1986) depicts a world in which sex-change operations are painless, inexpensive, and easily reversible. Ursula LeGuin (1969) describes an androgynous society in which individuals are sometimes female and sometimes male.

Judging from recent trends, some men will undoubtedly take on a larger share of domestic responsibility in the future, but some will just as undoubtedly reject family life entirely. For a society to achieve "egalitarian stability," three conditions must prevail: (1) women must earn as much or nearly as much as men; (2) men must do as much or nearly as much housework and childcare as women; and (3) the fertility rate must be high enough to sustain the population in the long run. The evidence in this book shows why it is unlikely that the combination of these three conditions will be met.

Persistent Disequilibrium

The most likely outcome over the next generation or two is a society with "persistent disequilibrium." The disequilibrium has two facets. First, if women emphasize careers—if they seek equality in the labor market—marriage and family are likely to continue to diminish in importance. The gains that women make in the labor market will continue to be offset by an increase in the need for them to support themselves and their children. Economic inequality will persist, especially for those women who have children. Second, even if most women and men reach an egalitarian accommodation which is stable for them personally, it is likely to be accompanied by a fertility rate so far below replacement level that the population as a whole will be in disequilibrium. This outcome is not inevitable, but seems more probable than any one of the other scenarios and as probable as all the others combined.

To be sure, the real world never plays out any single hypothetical scenario exactly as sketched. The future society may well contain elements of the four I have described; the characterizations and discussions should be understood as referring to the dominant form. Moreover, the future is, to some extent, in our own hands. By the policies that we choose in the next few years, we can have some influence on the direction our country takes.

Policy Recommendations

This book could end here. I am more a teacher than a preacher, more an analyst than a policymaker. I have been concerned more to understand what is going on than to judge it, more interested in conveying that understanding than in selling my own personal recommendations. Readers who have followed me this far, however, may want to know which policies I favor, and why.

My major recommendations take the form of three general principles rather than a detailed legislative agenda. They are:

1. Child-centered policies are preferable to labor market interventions.
2. The child-centered benefits should be widely available—not conditioned on marital status, employment status, or income.

3. The cost of the programs should be borne by the entire society through broad-based progressive taxes, not distributed
   through arbitrary methods with euphemistic names like "employer-provided" daycare.

My preference for child-centered policies over labor market interventions does not imply any desire to suspend or relax the laws
prohibiting discrimination at work. Indeed, I would extend such
prohibitions to other arenas such as sex-segregated clubs where
business and political affairs are discussed and, in effect, subsidized by government via tax-deductibility. But laws aimed at
curbing employer prejudice and exploitation cannot be expected
to have a large effect on occupational segregation or the wage gap
because employers are not the principal source of women's economic disadvantage.

To be sure, a nationwide system of administrative wage determination such as comprehensive comparable worth would nar-
row the economic gap between women and men. Such a policy,
however, would impose large real costs on the economy and
would seriously jeopardize the market system which is a key ele-
ment in our material prosperity and our political and social free-
doms. At a time when socialist countries such as the Soviet
Union and the People's Republic of China are finding it necessary to use markets and market-determined prices to allocate resources, it is alarming that some Americans would seriously urge
a major shift in the opposite direction.

The advocates of comparable worth are correct on one score:
society does put a lower value on the work that women do. But
they are incorrect in thinking that this results from some flaw in
the market. The market does what it is supposed to do—reflect
the preferences of those providing the demand for different types
of work and those providing the supply. For instance, why are
childcare workers poorly paid? Their low earnings are certainly
not the result of employer exploitation. The childcare industry is
highly competitive, and the dominant institutional form—family
daycare—is staffed by *self-employed* workers. It would be more

accurate to infer that the effective demand for childcare—that is, the willingness and ability to pay for it—is weak relative to the supply of childcare workers. This may be because men's preferences carry more weight than women's on the demand side of the market; men control a larger share of economic resources. If women's share were larger, and if women's preferences were different from men's, the market would quickly reflect that change in demand.

Historically, women have been disadvantaged in many ways—by law, by religion, by custom, and by prejudice. These handicaps are gradually being eliminated. In contemporary America, the greatest barrier to economic equality is children. Most women want to bear children and are concerned about their well-being once they are born. Whether this "maternal instinct" is primarily biological or some complex interaction of biology and culture, is not critical for framing public policy. What is important is that the "propensity to mother" is present and strong, and puts women at a disadvantage. I conclude that the fairest, most efficient, most effective way to help women is through their children.

Child-centered policies have another advantage: they help children directly. This appeals to my sense of equity because they are the group that has been most adversely affected by recent social and economic trends. The "feminization" of poverty, as we have seen, is largely illusory, at least for white women. But the "juvenilization" of poverty is very real for children of all races.

I also believe that policies that help children have significant positive externalities for society as a whole. When children are stunted physically, mentally, or emotionally, we all pay a price, and we all ought to be willing to bear some of the cost of raising the potential of the next generation. Even modest child allowances would move substantial numbers of children out of poverty.

Finally, these policies would provide a mild stimulus to fertility. I am not an ardent pronatalist, and I recognize the possibility that fertility may increase without any policy intervention. Many of our current policies, however, such as social security, have an antinatal effect; I would, therefore, like to see some restoration of balance that would move us closer to a replacement level of fertility.

In choosing among child-centered policies, I prefer a program such as child allowances for all mothers to one that provides benefits only if the mother is unmarried (or married), or only if the mother has a paid job (or does not have a paid job), or is conditioned on the family's income. It is possible that more sharply targeted programs would provide more benefits to children per dollar spent, but if the primary purpose is to reduce gender inequality, a broader approach is more appropriate.

We should favor policies that help mothers unconditionally over those that try to push them into one form of behavior or another. It is neither efficient nor equitable to discriminate against (or in favor of) women who want to stay home and care for their own children as opposed to those who want to take a paid job and buy childcare. Because I place a high value on allowing others to express their preferences, I do not want to use child allowances to impose my preferences on them.

My reluctance to vary the child allowances with family income stems from a different concern. If benefits are conditioned on income, the effect is to make the recipients face the equivalent of high marginal tax rates. This discourages parents from seeking better jobs or working harder at existing ones. If the child allowances were financed by an income tax, the program would, in effect, be income-conditioned, but the disincentive effects would be more widely diffused over the entire population. Again, it is important not to confuse goals. Child allowances financed by a proportional tax would result in a moderate amount of redistribution from rich to poor, but that is not the main objective of the policy.

Child allowances could have some flexibility, such as varying the size of the allowance with the age of the child. If, for instance, it is believed that the first year of life is very important and that some reduction in paid work by one or both parents is desirable, the allowance in the first year could be much higher than in subsequent years. This could have an effect similar to that of paid parental leave, but without many of the distortionary elements implicit in the latter approach. Paid parental leave is equivalent to providing a child allowance which is proportional to the parent's earnings—a very regressive subsidy. Furthermore, it denies any allowance to parents who do not have paid jobs, including those who are already at home in order to care for other children.

The decisions about the financing of child-centered policies are as important as the setting of conditions of eligibility. These policies impose two kinds of costs, transfer and real. The goals of the financing should be to distribute the transfer costs as equitably as possible and to keep the real costs as small as possible. A broad-based income or consumption tax meets both goals better than any other feasible scheme. The transfer burden is widely diffused throughout society on the basis of ability to pay. The real costs are largely limited to the disincentive effects of higher taxes on work and savings.

By contrast, attempts to finance child-centered programs through "employer-provided" benefits such as parental leave or subsidized daycare are likely to be more inequitable and induce more inefficiency. To be sure, any benefit that employers voluntarily provide because they believe it helps attract and keep good employees is unobjectionable. But compulsory employer-specific programs are usually less equitable than tax-supported ones because the transfer burden is not as widely diffused and not geared to ability to pay. It weighs more heavily on the consumers of particular products and on workers in particular industries—those who employ relatively more women of child-bearing age. The real costs also tend to be higher because programs imposed on employers change relative prices in arbitrary ways and induce inefficient shifts in behavior by firms and consumers.

One particularly pernicious fallacy is that child-centered programs imposed by legislation on the private sector would cost less than those funded through government. The former only appear less expensive because the cost gets mixed up with changes in wages and prices, whereas the public programs appear as explicit items in the budget.

Child allowances would certainly not solve all the problems of gender. Those women who are childless by choice or necessity would not benefit, except insofar as they would share in the positive externalities of a slightly higher fertility rate and more resources devoted to childcare. To the extent that child allowances make women more independent, the problem that many men have in coming to terms with that independence would be enlarged, but this is true of any policy that improves women's relative position.

It is their children that have made women vulnerable and dependent throughout the ages, and even today the demands of motherhood continue to take a great economic toll from women. Hasn't the time come for society to recognize this reality, to provide the resources that will simultaneously help women and their children?

Although the emphasis of this chapter is on public policies to help women, the role of private policy (in the broadest sense) should not be neglected. Individual firms, for instance, need to consider carefully the extent to which their own policies and procedures keep them from making fullest use of women in all types of work and at every level of responsibility. Stag social events, old-boy networks, mentoring, archaic nepotism rules, and a variety of other institutional practices not designed with evil intent may work simultaneously against the best interests of women and of the firm. Many firms may find that flex time, part-time jobs, and other accommodations to the reality of two-worker families will help them attract and hold desirable workers while also making a contribution to family and community life.

Individual women and men need to think through carefully what it is that they want out of life and what they need to do to reach their goals. Those women who are intent on successful careers should try to *signal* their intention and commitment as clearly as they can in order to blunt the impact of statistical discrimination. They can do this by the choices they make in school, by the jobs they take after graduation, and by their behavior on the job. They should seriously consider and seek out self-employment opportunities, commission jobs, and other forms of work where compensation is closely tied to individual performance.

In entering marriage, women and men should be honest with themselves as well as with each other about how much importance they attach to income, leisure, and children, and about the roles each spouse will play within the family. Many may reject the traditional division of labor in favor of an approach in which "both parents know the satisfaction of nurturing and earning and achieving," as urged in a *New York Times* editorial (November 17, 1987). But even in striving for a fifty-fifty marriage, it would be wise to be aware of two qualifications. First, it is unlikely that the spouses' contributions can always be equal. There will undoubtedly be times when one spouse "carries" the other; absent a willingness to do so, the marriage is likely to founder. Second, "fifty-fifty" need not mean that each spouse must do half of everything. Specialization need not be gender related, but the partnership gains strength from some division of labor based on innate or acquired skills in particular tasks.

Public policy and material conditions certainly help shape the choices people make, but in the end it is values and spirit that count the most. The low level of investment in America—both in capital goods and in children—may be partly the result of the tax and social security laws, but it also reflects a preoccupation with the present, a reluctance to make commitments to the future.

We can't go back to traditional roles and relationships, but we do need to arrest and reverse the fragmentation and fragility of family life. Our deepest problems are reflected not only in the Census Bureau statistics discussed in this book, but in much of contemporary literature. As a recent article on current fiction notes, "the self-obsessed characters have no history; rootless and disconnected, they are atomistic individuals calculating their self-interest . . . The men and women . . . appear to be parentless, conceived and raised to adulthood in a vacuum" (Lenz 1987, p. 37).

At bottom, it is this condition that most needs attention and this trend that most needs to be reversed. Can anything be done? Perhaps not, and that would be tragic. But it would be even more tragic if we refused to make an attempt.

References

Index

References

Astrachan, Anthony. 1986. *How Men Feel*. Garden City, N.Y.: Anchor Press/Doubleday.

Atrostic, B. K. 1983. "Alternative pay measures and labor market differentials." Bureau of Labor Statistics, Working Paper no. 127 (March).

Bander, Edward J. 1901/1981. *Mr. Dooley and Mr. Dunne: The Literary Life of a Chicago Catholic*. Charlottesville, Va.: Michie Company Law Publishers. Orig. pub. *Boston Globe,* June 9, 1901.

Bane, Mary Jo. 1986. "Household composition and poverty." In *Fighting Poverty: What Works and What Doesn't*, ed. S. H. Danziger and D. H. Weinberg. Cambridge, Mass.: Harvard University Press.

Barrett, Nancy. 1982. "Obstacles to economic parity for women." *American Economic Review Papers and Proceedings* 72 (May): 160–165.

Becker, Gary S. 1981. *A Treatise on the Family*. Cambridge, Mass.: Harvard University Press.

Becker, Gary S., and H. Gregg Lewis. 1973. "On the interaction between the quantity and quality of children." *Journal of Political Economy* 81, pt. 2 (March–April): S279–S288.

Beider, Perry C., B. Douglas Bernheim, Victor R. Fuchs, and John B. Shoven. Forthcoming. "Comparable worth in a general equilibrium model of the U.S. economy." In *Research in Labor Economics,* vol. 9, ed. Ronald G. Ehrenberg. Greenwich, Conn.: JAI Press.

Bianchi, Suzanne M., and Daphne Spain. 1986. *American Women in Transition*. New York: Russell Sage Foundation.

Blau, Francine D. 1977. *Equal Pay in the Office*. Lexington, Mass.: Lexington Books.

────── and Marianne A. Ferber. 1986. *The Economics of Women, Men, and Work*. Englewood Cliffs, N.J.: Prentice-Hall.

Bloom, David E. 1987. "Fertility timing, labor supply disruptions, and the wage profiles of American women." *Proceedings of the American Statistical Association*, Social Statistics Section.

────── and James Trussell. 1984. "What are the determinants of delayed childbearing and permanent childlessness in the United States?" *Demography* 21 (November): 591–611.

Blumstein, Philip, and Pepper Schwartz. 1983. *American Couples*. New York: William Morrow.

Brown, Helen Gurley. 1962. *Sex and the Single Girl*. New York: Pocket Books.

Brown, Judith K. 1970. "A note on the division of labor by sex." *American Anthropologist* 72 (October): 1073–78.

Brown, Roger. 1986. *Social Psychology: The Second Edition*. New York: Free Press.

Brozan, Nadine. 1987. "How the other half lives: A U.S.-Soviet study." *New York Times* (October 26): B8.

Cahn, Steven M. 1987. Letter to the editor. *New York Times* (October 29): 26.

Cohen, Joel E. 1987. "Making democratic babies. A review of Ben J. Wattenberg, *The Birth Dearth*." *The Wall Street Journal* (August 6): 20.

College Entrance Examination Board. 1977. *On Further Examination*. Report of the Advisory Panel on the Scholastic Aptitude Test Score Decline. New York: College Entrance Examination Board.

Commerce Clearing House, Inc. 1986. *Employment Practices Decisions*. Vol. 39. U.S. District Court, Northern District of Illinois, Eastern Division, Civil Action no. 79 C 4373, Feb. 4, 1986 (628F, Supp. 1264). A CCH Editorial Staff Publication, compiled from Labor Law Reports, Employment Practices, nos. 267–274. 4025 W. Peterson Ave., Chicago, Ill. 60646.

Davidson, Sara. 1984. "Having it all." *Esquire* (June): 54–60.

de Beauvoir, Simone. 1949/1961. *The Second Sex.* Tr. H. M. Parshley. New York: Bantam Books. Orig. pub. in French, 1949.

Demeny, Paul. 1986. "Population and the invisible hand." *Demography* 23 (November): 473–487.

Dietz, William H., Jr., and Steven L. Gortmaker. 1985. "Do we fatten our children at the television set? Obesity and television viewing in children and adolescents." *Pediatrics* 75 (May): 807–812.

Easterlin, Richard A. 1987. *Birth and Fortune.* 2nd ed. Ch. 10, "The struggle for relative economic status." Chicago: University of Chicago Press.

———— 1980. *Birth and Fortune: The Impact of Numbers on Personal Welfare.* New York: Basic Books.

Ephron, Nora. 1983. *Heartburn.* New York: Knopf.

Festinger, L. 1957. *A Theory of Cognitive Dissonance.* Evanston, Ill.: Row, Peterson.

Fleming, Anne Taylor. 1986. "The American Wife." *New York Times Magazine* (October 26): 29ff.

Frank, Robert H. 1978. "Why women earn less: The theory and estimation of differential over-qualification." *American Economic Review* 68 (June): 360–373.

Friedan, Betty. 1987. *New York Times.* "The Weekend Review," sect. 4, p. 1. March 29.

———— 1963. *The Feminine Mystique.* New York: Norton.

Fuchs, Victor R. 1986a. *The Health Economy.* Cambridge, Mass.: Harvard University Press.

———— 1986b. "Sex differences in economic well-being." *Science* 32 (April 25): 459–464.

———— 1986c. "Why are children poor?" National Bureau of Economic Research, Working Paper no. 1984. July.

———— 1983. *How We Live.* Cambridge, Mass.: Harvard University Press.

———— 1974. *Who Shall Live? Economics, Health, and Social Choice.* New York: Basic Books.

———— 1971. "Differences in hourly earnings between men and women." *Monthly Labor Review* (May): 9–15.

————, ed. 1969. *Production and Productivity in the Service Industries.* Conference on Research in Income and Wealth, vol. 34. New

York: Columbia University Press, for the National Bureau of Economic Research.

——— 1968. *The Service Economy.* New York: National Bureau of Economic Research.

——— and Joyce Jacobsen. 1986. "Employee response to compulsory short-time work." National Bureau of Economic Research, Working Paper no. 2089.

Furstenberg, Frank F., Jr., and Gretchen A. Condran. 1988. "Family change and adolescent well-being: A reexamination of U.S. trends." In *Family Change and Public Policy,* ed. Andrew J. Cherlin. Washington, D.C., Urban Institute Press.

Genevie, Louis E., and Eva Margolies. 1987. *The Motherhood Report.* New York: Macmillan.

Gold, Michael Evan. 1983. *A Dialogue on Comparable Worth.* Ithaca, N.Y.: ILR Press, New York State School of International and Labor Relations, Cornell University.

Goldin, Claudia. 1986. "The economic status of women in the early republic: Quantitative evidence." *Journal of Interdisciplinary History* 16 (Winter): 375–404.

Gortmaker, Steven L., William H. Dietz, Jr., Arther M. Sobol, and Cheryl A. Wehler. 1987. "Increasing pediatric obesity in the United States." *American Journal of Diseases of Children* 141 (May): 535–540.

Harris, Louis. 1987. *Inside America.* New York: Vintage Books.

Hartmann, Heidi. 1976. "Capitalism, patriarchy, and job segregation by sex." In *Women and the Work Place,* ed. Martha Blaxall and Barbara Reagan. Chicago: University of Chicago Press.

Healthcare Forum. 1987. "Sexual static," a conversation with authors Morton H. Shaevitz and Marjorie Hansen Shaevitz. (May–June): 25–30.

Herrnstein, Richard J. 1985. "Are women workers different?" *Fortune* 111 (April 1): 177.

Hoem, Britta, and Jan M. Hoem. 1986. "One child is not enough: Who has a second and third child in modern Sweden?" Paper presented at the annual meeting of the Population Association of America, San Francisco. April 3–5.

Jacobsen, Joyce. 1987. "Differences in occupational mix and hourly earnings by sex and race between the public and private sectors." Stanford University, work in progress.

Johansson, S. Ryan. 1987. "Status anxiety and demographic contraction of privileged populations." *Population and Development Review* 13 (September): 439–470.

Johnson, George, and Gary Solon. 1986. "Estimates of the direct effects of comparable worth policy." *American Economic Review* 76 (December): 1117–25.

Johnston, Lloyd D., Patrick M. O'Malley, and Jerald G. Bachman. 1984. *Drugs and American High School Students, 1975–83.* National Institute on Drug Abuse, Public Health Service. DHHS Publication no. (ADM)85–1374.

Jong, Erica. 1983. "Twenty years later." *Barnard Alumnae Magazine* (Summer): 2–4.

Joshi, Heather. 1986. Quoted in *The Economist* (July 19): 43.

——— and Marie-Louise Newell. 1987. "Family responsibilities and pay differentials: Evidence for men and women born in 1946." Discussion Paper no. 157 (March). London: Centre for Economic Policy Research.

Kahne, Hilda. 1985. *Reconceiving Part-Time Work.* Totowa, N.J.: Rowman and Allanheld.

Kaplan, Mordecai. 1957. *Basic Values in Jewish Religion.* New York: Reconstructionist Press.

LeGuin, Ursula K. 1969. *The Left Hand of Darkness.* New York: Ace Books.

Leigh, J. Paul. 1983. "Sex differences in absenteeism." *Industrial Relations* 22 (Fall): 349–361.

Lenz, Elinor. 1987. "The generation gap: From Persephone to Portnoy." *New York Times Book Review* (August 30): 1, 36–37.

Levy, Frank. 1987. *Dollars and Dreams.* New York: Russell Sage Foundation.

Maccoby, Eleanor E. 1987. Personal communication (October 23).

——— and Carol Nagy Jacklin. 1987. "Gender segregation in childhood." In *Advances in Child Development and Behavior,* vol. 20. Ed. Hayne Reese. New York: Academic Press.

Maccoby, Eleanor E., Robert H. Mnookin, and Charlene E. Depner. 1986. "Post-divorce families: Custodial arrangements compared." Paper presented at meeting of the American Association for the Advancement of Science, Philadelphia. May.

Manning, W. G., J. P. Newhouse, N. Duan, E. G. Keeler, A. Leibowitz, and M. S. Marquis. 1987. "Health insurance and the demand for medical care: Evidence from a randomized experiment." *American Economic Review* 77 (June): 251–277.

Mead, Margaret. 1952. *Male and Female*. New York: William Morrow.

Millett, Kate. 1970. *Sexual Politics*. Garden City, N.Y.: Doubleday.

Mincer, Jacob. 1962. "Labor force participation of married women: A study of labor supply." In *Aspects of Labor Economics*. Princeton, N.J.: National Bureau of Economic Research and Princeton University Press.

Moore, Kristin A., and Isabel V. Sawhill. 1976. "Implications of women's employment for home and family life." In *Women and the American Economy: A Look to the 1980s,* ed. Juanita M. Kreps. Englewood Cliffs, N.J.: Prentice-Hall.

Moorman, Jeanne E., and Arthur J. Norton. 1987. "Current trends in marriage and divorce among American women." *Journal of Marriage and the Family* 49 (February): 3–14.

Murdock, George P., and Caterina Provost. 1973. "Factors in the division of labor by sex: A cross-cultural analysis." *Ethnology* 12 (April): 203–225.

Myers, David E., Ann Milne, Fran Ellman, and Alan Ginsburg. 1983. "Single parents, working mothers and the educational achievement of secondary school age children." Paper presented at the annual meeting of the American Educational Research Association, Montreal, Canada. April.

Myrdal, Gunnar. 1987. "Utilitarianism and modern economics." In *Arrow and the Foundations of the Theory of Economic Policy,* ed. George R. Feiwel. New York: New York University Press.

National Institute of Mental Health. 1982. *Television and Behavior: Ten Years of Scientific Progress and Implications for the Eighties.* Vol. 1, summary report. Washington, D.C.: U.S. Government Printing Office.

Newsweek. 1978. "Teen-age suicide." Vol. 92 (August 28): 74–77.

New York Times. 1987. January 4, p. 19.

New York Times. 1987. June 29, p. B1.

New York Times. 1987. November 17, editorial page.

Nimick, Ellen H., Howard N. Snyder, Dennis P. Sullivan, and Nancy J. Tierney. 1982. *Juvenile Court Statistics.* National Center for Juvenile Justice (U.S. Department of Justice), 701 Forbes Ave., Pittsburgh, Pa. 15219.

Northern California Jewish Bulletin. 1987. March, p. 16.

O'Connell, Martin, and David E. Bloom. 1987. "Juggling jobs and babies: America's child care challenge." *Population Trends and Public Policy* 12 (February): 1–16. Occasional Paper no. 12, Population Reference Bureau, Inc., P.O. Box 96152, Washington, D.C. 20090.

Paffenbarger, Ralph S., Jr., Stanley H. King, and Alvin L. Wing. 1969. "Characteristics in youth that predispose to suicide and accidental death in later life." *American Journal of Public Health* 59 (June): 900–908.

Pearce, Diana, and Harriette McAdoo. 1984. "Women and children: Alone and in poverty." In *Families and Change: Social Needs and Public Policies,* ed. Rosalie G. Genovese. New York: Praeger.

Perlez, Jane. 1987. "Banks' job program fails to find enough qualified students." *New York Times* (June 29): B1.

Pet Food Institute. 1986. "Fact sheet." Washington, D.C.

Phelps, Edmund S. 1972. "The statistical theory of racism and sexism." *American Economic Review* 62 (September): 659–661.

Pomeroy, Sarah B. 1984. *Women in Hellenistic Egypt*. New York: Schocken Books.

Price, Lucien. 1954. *Dialogues of Alfred North Whitehead*. Boston: Little, Brown.

Principal. 1980. "One-parent families and their children: The schools' most significant minority." Vol. 60 (September): 31–37.

Quindlen, Anna. 1987. Column. *New York Times,* April 29.

Reinhold, Robert. 1987. "California tries caring for its growing ranks of latchkey children." *New York Times* (October 4): 4.

Reskin, Barbara F., and Heidi I. Hartmann, eds. 1986. *Women's Work, Men's Work: Sex Segregation on the Job*. Washington, D.C.: National Academy Press.

Sanday, Peggy Reeves. 1981. *Female Power and Male Dominance*. Cambridge: Cambridge University Press.

Savvy. 1987. Letter to the editor from Elizabeth Evory Green. June, p. 19.

Sen, Amartya. 1985. "Social choice and justice: A review article." *Journal of Economic Literature* 23 (December): 1764–76.

Simpson, Janice C. 1987. "A shallow labor pool spurs businesses to act to bolster education." *Wall Street Journal* (September 28): 1.

Stafford, Frank P. 1987. "Women's work, sibling competition, and children's school performance." University of Michigan, Institute for Social Research, Working Paper no. 8036. April.

Steinem, Gloria. 1987. *Ms.* Magazine (July–August): 55.

Sweden Now. 1986. "A land where father (sometimes) is left holding the baby." No. 6, pp. 27–28.

Tannahill, Reay. 1980. *Sex in History.* New York: Stein & Day. Rpt. Scarborough Books, 1982.

Teitelbaum, Michael S., and Jay M. Winter. 1985. *The Fear of Population Decline.* New York: Academic Press.

Theroux, Phyllis. 1987. *NightLights.* New York: Viking Press.

Tolstoy, Leo. 1986. *Diaries.* Ed. and tr. R. F. Christian. New York: Scribners.

Uhlenberg, Peter, and David Eggebeen. 1986. "The declining well-being of American adolescents." *The Public Interest* 82 (Winter): 25–38.

U.S. Bureau of the Census. 1987. *Who's Minding the Kids? Child Care Arrangements: Winter 1984–85.* Current Population Reports, ser. P–70, no. 9. Washington, D.C.: U.S. Government Printing Office.

—— 1987. *Statistical Abstract of the United States: 1987.* 107th ed., p. 162. Washington, D.C.: U.S. Government Printing Office.

—— 1986 and 1980. *Current Population Survey, March: Annual Demographic File Technical Documentation.* Washington, D.C.: U.S. Government Printing Office.

—— 1980 and 1960. *Census of Population and Housing: Public-Use Microdata Samples Technical Documentation.* Washington, D.C.: U.S. Government Printing Office.

U.S. Commission on Civil Rights. 1985. *Comparable Worth: An Analysis and Recommendations.* Washington, D.C.: U.S. Commission on Civil Rights.

U.S. Congress. 1987. *Educational Achievement: Explanations and Implications of Recent Trends.* Prepared by Daniel M. Koretz. August. Washington, D.C.: Congressional Budget Office.

Varley, John. 1986. *Blue Champagne.* New York: Berkeley Books.

—— 1980. *Picnic on Nearside.* New York: Berkeley Books.

von Hipple, Theodor Gottlieb. 1792. *On Improving the Status of Women.* Ed. and tr. Timothy F. Sellner. Detroit: Wayne State University Press, 1979.

Wald, Michael. 1987. Personal communication, December 11.

Wall Street Journal. 1986. December 9, p. 1.

Warburton, Dorothy. 1987. "Reproductive loss: How much is preventable?" *New England Journal of Medicine* 316 (January 15): 158–160.

Wattenberg, Ben J. 1987. *The Birth Dearth.* New York: Pharos Books.

Wellesley Class of 1966. 1986. *The Record Book for the Twentieth Reunion.* Wellesley, Mass.: Wellesley College.

West, Rebecca. 1987. Quoted in "Suburban Classic" by Leslie Garis, in *Ms.* Magazine (July–August): 142.

Wills, Geoffrey, and Tom Cooke. 1983. *A Friend for Frances.* Beverly, Mass.: Parker Brothers.

Winn, Marie. 1983. *Children Without Childhood.* New York: Penguin Books.

Wollstonecraft, Mary. 1792. *Vindication of the Rights of Women.* London. Rpt. New York: Dert & Dutton, 1929.

Zill, Nicholas. 1987. "Behavior, achievement, and health problems among children in stepfamilies: Findings from a national survey of child health." In *The Impact of Divorce, Single Parenting, and Step-Parenting on Children,* ed. E. Mavis Hetherington and J. Arasteh. Forthcoming.

Index